THE pROpHECiES
OF ST. MALACHY

Introduction and Commentary by Peter Bander

TAN BOOKS AND PUBLISHERS, INC.
Rockford, Illinois 61105

Library of Congress Catalog Card Number: 74-125419

ISBN: 0-89555-038-5

Originally published in 1969 by Colin Smythe, Ltd., Gerrards Cross, Buckinghamshire, England under the title *The Prophecies of St. Malachy and St. Columbkille.*

Originally published in the United States by Alba House, Division of the Society of St. Paul, Staten Island, New York in 1970 under the title *The Prophecies of St. Malachy.*

PRINTED AND BOUND IN THE UNITED STATES OF AMERICA

TAN BOOKS AND PUBLISHERS, INC.
P. O. Box 424
Rockford, Illinois 61105
1973

FOREWORD

In publishing THE PROPHECIES OF ST MALACHY Colin Smythe Limited have produced an instructive and entertaining book.

There is a great deal of instant information in Peter Bander's nutshell biographical accounts of the popes who occupied the Roman See since the year 1143 to our present time — and indeed of the antipopes as well. The remarkable way in which the visions St Malachy is alleged to have had are shown to apply to the successive individual popes is most amusing. Is it not the case to repeat: "Se non è vero, è ben trovato"?

Whatever one may think of the genuineness of the prophecies attributed to St Malachy, here is a fascinating study which provides the curious reader with much profit and pleasure.

ARCHBISHOP H. E. CARDINALE
Apostolic Nuncio to Belgium and Luxembourg
until recently Apostolic Delegate to Great Britain

PREFACE

If this book does no more than give pause to those scoffers who customarily go about saying that the Prophecies of Malachy are nothing other than scurrilous rubbish, it will have accomplished a great deal — if only because there are so many people who tend to think this way. There is another group, of course, who have never heard of these famous foretellings of the popes by which the good Malachy undertook to list in advance the proper succession of Roman pontiffs from Celestine II (1143) to "the end of the world." He didn't just come right out and name them, of course. That would have taken all the sport out of it for one thing and, for another, would have considerably curtailed the free will of the College of Cardinals. Quite sensibly, he chose to reveal the successors under symbolic titles, set down in Latin.

I belong to yet a third group — or belonged, I should say — who had heard of the Prophecies but had not bothered to think much about their validity one way or the other. I could, as so many of my contemporary indifferentists are wont to say, not have cared less. But count me now among the utterly concerned and utterly converted. Peter Bander's commentary and interpretation of the prophecies have carried the day completely. So far as I'm concerned, there's not the least shadow of a doubt as to their authenticity.

The scoffers, of course, begin with the primary objection that these writings were not even "discovered" for some four-hundred odd years after Malachys' death in the year 1148. They object further that he would surely have told somebody about them, at least his death friend St. Bernard of Clairvaux; they carp and twitter and nit-pick in other disagreeable and tendentious ways as well. But to no avail — the elegant and soaring scholarship of Peter Bander disposes of all these objections with authoritative dispatch. He remains too much the professional even to descend to the gut-level argument that I, laboring under no such restraining ethic, would have cited at once: namely, that Malachy was not only Irish, but an Irish saint, and the first Irishman to actually be canonized by formal process of the Church. Would such a man be apt to jeopardize his chances by leaving a notorious piece of scurrilous writing behind him?

There will be those, too, who say that it's easy enough to match up pope and prophetic clue after the fact. Thus we now know that when

Malachy wrote *Bos Albanus in Portu* that he was obviously referring to Rodrigo Borgia, Alexander VI (1492-1503), because of "the pope's armorial bearings and his Cardinal titles of Albano and Porto." He also behaved like a bull on more than a few occasions so that the prediction "the Alban bull at the port" is not only literally but allegorically accurate. But the wicked Alexander is grossly obvious; it takes a knowledge of the papacy amounting almost to an obsession — albeit a most lofty one — to realize that *Picus Inter Escas* (A woodpecker among the food) was going to turn out to be Nicholas IV.

Interest in the prophecies is somewhat cyclical in nature, tending to go up sharply when the reigning pontiff grows extremely old or falls dangerously ill. Before and during actual conclaves it is next to impossible to lay your hands on a copy. Peter Bander's interpretations, filled as they are with the highly condensed soup of scholarship as well as with the lightning flashes of nearly pure inspiration, should soon be recognized as *the* authoritative version and will doubtless be in sharp demand.

Which makes me admire all the more the modesty of Peter Bander, who, having forged such a masterwork of authenticity can then step humbly aside and say, as he does in his introduction, that the reader need not "extend to them the same reverence you may extend to the Gospels."

Reverence no; but profound respect, certainly. Only once did the author strain my credulity and that so slightly as to be virtually insignificant. He circulates the rumor that during the conclave which was to elect John XXIII, a certain Cardinal from the United States, evidently having taken Malachy's forecast that the next pope would be "pastor and mariner" literally, rented a boat, filled it with sheep and sailed thus conspicuously up and down the Tiber. Pope John, of course, as bishop of Venice, had the maritime claim nailed down.

What disturbs me and should disturb the reader to an equal degree is that after "Flower of Flowers," that is to say after Paul VI, there are only three more prophecies. Whoever he turns out to be, *Petrus Romanus* will be the last. Time is running out. It's later than we all think. The end of the world is at hand. If Malachy and Peter Bander say it's going to happen, then happen it surely will.

Joel Wells
Editor, *The Critic*

PUBLISHER'S PREFACE

The present book was originally published by Colin Smythe, Limited, of Gerrards Cross, England in 1969 under the title *The Prophecies of St. Malachy and St. Columbkille.* In 1970 Alba House, a Division of the Society of St. Paul, Staten Island, New York, with the permission of Colin Smythe, Limited, brought out a hardbound edition of *The Prophecies of St. Malachy* only. That edition having gone out of print toward the end of 1972, and Alba House electing not to reprint, we negotiated with the original publisher to issue the book once more. We also have chosen to reprint only *The Prophecies of St. Malachy* because they form a unified subject matter; those of St. Columbkille (521-597) cover a longer period of time, concern many unrelated subjects, and are difficult to read and more difficult to understand (even with the help of Mr. Bander's footnotes). Added to this, they distract, in our opinion, from the powerful import of St. Malachy's prophecies.

The over-riding value of the present little volume is twofold: These prophecies are extremely accurate, and there are only four more, after Pope Paul VI, yet to be fulfilled (according to the prophecies) before the End of Time. Mr. Bander has compiled here an inestimably valuable tract in the field of prophecy because the prophecies of St. Malachy fit beautifully into a pattern woven from the various saintly prognostications, the sibylline oracles, quasi-secular and folk predictions, and Biblical prophecy. This pattern becomes highly discernible upon a reading of such recent works as *The Book of Destiny* (1955), *Prophecy for Today* (1956), *Catholic Prophecy* (1970), *History of Antichrist* (1968), *The Prophets and Our Times* (1943), and *The Reign of the Antichrist* (1951). The present volume, in adding weight and credence to the prophecies of St. Malachy, at the same time further develops and enlarges the picture we gain from these other sources about the times we live in and the events, it would seem, we are about to witness.

All of these works have conspired to educate the Catholic readership on the value and consolation of prophecy study. Our attempt with this work is to further serious study of prophecy ("Despise not prophecies." I *Thes.* 5:20) and thereby to encourage a wider and a deeper study of the entirety of our Faith. By presenting an inexpensive edition we would hope to reach that many more people and trust that the format will not detract, in the reader's mind, from the scholarship that has entered into the work.

Whereas Mr. Bander's book is not a definitive treatment of these prophecies, it certainly is the best available at the present time; and anyone (perhaps the author himself) wishing to pursue matters further will certainly have to take full cognizance of this work. In any event, the field of Catholic prophetic research (and there exists such a field, though the reader may yet be unfamiliar with even a modicum of the plethora of material) owes Mr. Bander several significant debts. Besides his thrusting these prophecies before our view, he has supplied sufficient historical data with each epigram to *substantiate the validity of the entire series.* Though in a few particular instances the significance is not clear, he points out, however, that our not seeing the meaning does not prove it is not there, our knowledge of a given Pope being undoubtedly too deficient to enlighten us. Added to this, he has made two excellent contributions toward interpreting the last four prophecies; namely, he has suggested that "*De Medietate Lunae*" ("Of the Half of the Moon") could well indicate a Pope reigning during a time of strife with the Moslems; this is exactly the conclusion of Mr. Dupont in *Catholic Prophecy* (TAN, 1970), who cites other prophecies by saints to the effect that Europe will once again be invaded by the followers of Mohammed, this during a period of civil war in Europe that leaves her weak and defenseless. Concerning "*Gloria Olivae*" ("The Glory of the Olive"), Mr. Bander has made a decided contribution by pointing out that the Order of St. Benedict is otherwise known as the "Olivetans" and that their tradition holds that this Pope will be of their order. Mr. Dupont's conclusions reinforce still others of Mr. Bander regarding "*Gloria Olivae*," for this would seem to be none other than that miraculously designated Pope who, after a horrible period of world turmoil, will, by his exemplary holiness, convert masses of people and leaders of nations to the Roman Catholic Church, it being during his pontificate that there will be "one fold and one shepherd." (*Jn.* 10:16).

We trust the reader will excuse these somewhat substantive discussions, which, though generally not the role of a publisher, will, it is hoped, prove instructive and give a frame of reference for the present volume. The *Prophecies of St. Malachy* certainly do fit into a broad background of what we now know about the future, and though of limited content are of powerful import. To this we would like to add our special thanks to Colin Smythe, Limited, for permitting us to reissue this illuminating book.

Thomas A. Nelson
March 20, 1973

THE PROPHECIES OF MALACHY

The prophecies of Malachy have almost come to an end; just three more popes and *De medietate lunæ, De labore solis* and *Gloria olivæ* will have joined the other 108 pontiffs thus anticipated or prophesied by Malachy. For three more pontifical reigns to come, some people will speculate as to the possible identity of the next pope and, after each conclave the interpreters will have a field day. The Benedictine historian Arnold Wion was the first to mention these prophecies in his book *Lignum Vitæ,* published in 1559. With the briefest of introductions he inserted them after an equally brief summary of St Malachy's life. Since then a never ending controversy about the authenticity and authorship of the prophecies has led to many new editions and publications of the same, each trying to prove the author's personal belief. In the seventeenth century Father Menestrier, a famous Jesuit, put forward his hypothesis that these prophecies had originated in 1590 during the conclave which resulted in Gregory XIV becoming the elected pontiff. Fr. Menestrier goes as far as naming the forger; a member of Cardinal Simoncelli's party is supposed to have forged these prophecies in order to influence the electors in favour of his Cardinal who was the doyen of the Sacred College and, by virtue of his office and other qualities, surely a favourite for the pontificate. Cardinal Simoncelli was Bishop of Orvieto, his birthplace, and the motto given to him in the prophecies, *Ex antiquitate urbis,* is simply an allusion to Orvieto (*Latin: Urbs vetus*). Perhaps it is fair to add that Fr. Menestrier does not furnish us with evidence to substantiate his accusation. In 1871 Abbé Cucherat put forward his hypothesis; Malachy had his visions between the end of 1139 and the beginning of 1140 during his visit to Rome. He committed the visions to paper and handed the manuscript to Pope Innocent II to comfort the Holy Father in his afflictions. Innocent II placed the manuscript in the archives where they remained unread for nearly four centuries. Unfortunately Abbé Cucherat does not supply his evidence either. If we were to place the works of those who have repudiated the Prophecies of Malachy on scales and balance them against those who have accepted them, we would probably reach a fair equilibrium; however, the most important factor, namely the popularity of the prophecies, particularly among the ordinary people (as distinct from scholars), makes them as relevant to the second half of the twentieth century as they have ever been. St Malachy's family name was O'Morgair and he was born in Armagh, Ireland, in 1094, almost one thousand years ago. He was baptised in Maelmhaedhoc (this name has been Latinized as Malachy) and he studied under Imhar O'Hagan who later became the Abbot of Armagh. In 1119 he was ordained priest by St Cellach (Celsus), studied under St Malchus and in 1123 he was elected Abbot of Bangor. His spectacular career had not ended; a year later he was consecrated Bishop of Connor and in 1132 he became Primate of Armagh. However, owing to intrigues, he had to wait two years before he could finally take posesssion of the See of Armagh; even then he had to purchase the Bachal Isu (staff of Jesus) from Niall, the usurping lay-primate. He died in 1148 at Clairvaux in the arms of St Bernard.

Unlike the life of many saints, that of St Malachy is well documented because his contemporary, St Bernard of Clairvaux, acted as his biographer at the request of the Abbot of Mellifont.

St Bernard describes Malachy as distinguished for his meekness, humility, obedience, modesty and as truly diligent in his studies. He also tells us at length of Malachy foretelling the day and hour of his death. The Breviary in its office for the festival of St Malachy mentions that he was enriched with the gift of prophecy.

The interested reader who wishes to study the life of St Malachy in greater depth and detail may wish to read any of the numerous life stories which have been written. In the second half of the last century Malachy's prophecies concerning the popes were widely read and studied in Ireland; it is therefore not surprising to find some detailed accounts of the Saint's life written in those years.

Since St Malachy left his prophecies concerning the popes of the Catholic Church behind, some 900 years ago, there have been many interpreters and probably as many critics who have in their own way tried to make these prophecies palatable to the reader or denounce them as forgeries.

Two objections to the prophecies most critics have in common are first, the silence of St Bernard on the subject, and secondly the tortuous methods employed by some of Malachy's interpreters in applying the various prophecies to certain popes.

The fact that St Bernard of Clairvaux does not refer to the prophecies and catalogue them among Malachy's other writings simply confirms to me that his character assessment of the Saint which describes Malachy as humble, meek and modest, was true to form.

Bearing in mind the nature of Malachy's prophecies, one sees soon that they do not conform to the pattern of Old and New Testament prophecies; they are not warnings of imminent dangers or threats to mankind; they do not point to any actual disaster (not really, because the destruction of Rome is 112 Popes ahead of his time!). There is no guidance, just a monotonous litany of Latin words or phrases, each symbolising a successive pope.

The second criticism against Malachy's vision concerns the tortuous methods adopted by some interpreters in applying them to some of the Popes. In the case of Clement XI (1700-1721) to whom Malachy had given the motto *Flores circumdati* (surrounded with flowers), his followers even struck a medal during his reign which bore this motto. After all, Malachy's prophecies have been publicly known since 1559 and it is reasonable to assume that those who designed the medal knew of them.

However, it is fair to say that the vast majority of Malachy's predictions about successive Popes is amazingly accurate — always remembering that he gives only a minimum of information.

The first three pontiffs mentioned in his vision, *Ex castro Tiberis, Inimicus expulsus* and *Ex magnitudine montis* were Celestine II, Lucius II and Eugene III; their respective reigns, 1143-1144, 1144-1145 and 1145-1153 fell within the life time of Malachy.

Circumstantial evidence points, therefore, to a time before 1143 when Malachy had his visions. His visit to Pope Innocent II in 1139 appears to have resulted in unfulfilled requests; the Pope refused to grant Malachy permission to spend the remainder of his life at the monastery of Clairvaux; he promised to grant Malachy the Pallium for the diocese of Armagh and Tuam (a See lately erected by Celsus) but failed to keep his promise.

Perhaps it was Malachy's preoccupation with the Papacy, that sparked off his visions. Who knows? Perhaps he was given the privilege of seeing before him the long line of popes to come, the timelessness of his Church, the strife and struggle during the period of antipopes, until finally Petrus Romanus will reign and feed his flock amid tribulations.

Some interpreters have suggested that Malachy does not specifically mention that no other pope would reign between *Gloria olivæ* (no. 111) and *Petrus Romanus*, who will be the last (given as no. 112); they suppose that Malachy just gave the next one thousand years and then mentioned the last pope to bring his prophecies to a conclusion. Far be it from me to join them in their speculations.

We have now reached *Flos florum;* Pope Paul VI has indeed *Flos florum,* the Fleur-de-Lis in his coat of arms. Out of 92 popes whose arms are published by the Vatican, Pope Paul VI is the thirteenth with such a bearing. In some cases there appears to be a discrepancy between the arms published by the Vatican and those given by Panvinio. Those coats of arms published by the Vatican and reproduced in this book are of course the papal crests; Panvinio tends to refer to the family coat of arms of the particular pope. These two are often quite different and bear no relation to one another. For example Clement IV, described by Malachy as *Draco depressus* (The dragon crushed) is given a coat of arms with six Fleurs-de-Lis; Panvinio describes his arms as an 'eagle clawing a dragon', which is almost tailor-made for the prophecy.

I have so far refused to be drawn into any speculation or interpretation; yet, in the course of my brief research on this fascinating subject I have pondered on one who is yet to come. I don't know whether it will be during my own life on earth, or if I will have my curiosity satisfied elsewhere. The Pope who will reign under the motto *De labore solis* arouses my special interest. In 1856 one interpreter, who signs himself 'a son of St Jarbath', is not quite sure how to translate this Latin legend. He cannot find any explanation if he were to

translate it as 'of the labouring sun', and so he tells us that *De labore solis* obviously refers to an eclipse of the sun, quoting from Matthew 24 (29) —
"The sun shall be darkened and the moon shall not give her light".

Somehow I cannot envisage any more pontiffs in Rome when Jesus' prophecies concerning the end of the world come true; what about *Gloria olivæ* and *Petrus Romanus*? — Perhaps *De labore solis* is yet another allusion to armorial bearings. Is it not possible that among us is already a young priest or even bishop who has the sun in his coat of arms?

On the other hand, astronomers are in a position to tell us about future eclipses of the sun, and the election of a pope in the year of such an eclipse might be another explanation. A prophecy is a prediction of future events which cannot be foreseen and for which there are no reasonable causes to be brought about. Unlike the study of form in horse-racing or other sporting events which may create certain odds for or against 'forecasts', here we have no form to study. The only way we can possibly consider a prophecy genuine or false is to wait for the prophesied event to come about as foretold, or not.

We have one comfort: experience has shown that the Holy Ghost tends to work in spite of our meddling in all possible matters, and also quite independently of prophecies and interpreters; He even is known to have worked in the conclave in spite of heavy opposition from Princes of the Church. It is therefore reasonable to assume that if the Holy Ghost who inspired St Malachy is the same one who inspires the electors, he would fulfil the prophecies as well.

One of the strong objections against the prophecies of Malachy in certain Catholic circles appears to be the fact that among the successive popes mentioned, appear the reference to the antipopes. Although two of them are clearly marked as schismatic, *Corvus Schismaticus* — the schismatic crow, and *Schisma Barchinonicum* — (he was a Canon of Barcelona), the others take their place among the legitimate popes without any special mention of their peculiar position.

I consider those objections quite unreasonable from people who accept that Judas Iscariot was one of the Apostles of Jesus and do not object to the many biblical characters who were called but never chosen. After all, these antipopes are historical characters, they all held high episcopal offices before claiming the supreme title to the see of St Peter and, they were, within limits, accepted as real popes by a large section of Catholic followers; the fact that events proved them wrong or even schismatic does not belittle the important function and position they commanded at the time. Giacconius, who in his commentary on Malachy's prophecies only lists the canonically elected popes, quarrels with Panvinio for ranking popes and antipopes next to one another. This great Schism in the Catholic Church, when popes and antipopes existed side by side, lasted for almost three centuries. St Antonius himself comments on this and points out that much is written by different parties in defence of the one or the other ecclesiastical dignitary. All sides were well defended by excellent theologians and Canon Lawyers, and in the end, the argument was settled by establishing the rightful successor of St Peter as the one who was canonically elected to the supreme office. St Antonius goes further by saying that the ordinary people could not possibly participate in such difficult and delicate discussion as they did not understand Canon Law; they followed the advice and guidance of their spiritual fathers and superiors. Personally, I consider the fact that antipopes are included in the list as a point in favour of Malachy.

Finally, the language of Malachy. Many a critic has commented on the use of Latin — or should I say the misuse of Latin by Malachy. This also has been brought into the argument about the authenticity of the prophecies. There are many different translations of the Latin descriptions, often confusingly different. For example, the scholar whom I mentioned before and who signs himself a 'son of St Jarbath', relies heavily on Wion; he translates *De schola exiet* (Pope Clement III, 1187-1191): "he shall go forth from the school". The Revd. Ailbe J. Luddy, O.Cist., in his excellent book *Life of Malachy*, translates the same phrase: "he will come out of a school". Such examples occur time and time again and it becomes obvious, even to the person who can speak little or no Latin, that in its original usage only one meaning could have been implied. However, one cannot entirely rule out the possibility of ambiguity by the writer of the prophecies, although I am inclined to look for faults among the interpreters; in a way it does not matter at all, Malachy will neither gain nor lose by a wrong translation or interpretation.

I have discussed the prophecies of Malachy with many friends, among them Bishops, Archbishops and high prelates of the Roman Catholic Church, the Church of England and the Church of Ireland. We have always enjoyed our conversations and the tremendous sense of humour emanating from them. With no disrespect to the Saint, we have laughed at our personal idiosyncrasies in making certain Latin verses fit certain eminent dignitaries we knew, but most of all, we have realised that we shall still have to wait some time before we really know whether St Malachy has once again foiled our speculations, or if, perchance, one of us has been right. My advice to the reader of the following comments on St Malachy's prophecies is simple: please, do not extend to them the same reverence you may extend to the Gospels, and remember that to err is human, but to err too often is foolish.

Although the theory that the prophecies of Malachy might be 16th century forgeries has been put forward from time to time, it is of particular interest that one of the most respectable and outstanding historians of the 16th century seems to have accepted them completely. Onofrio Panvinio, who had turned down episcopal honours, became corrector and reviser of the Vatican Library in 1556. Most interpreters of Malachy rely on his "Epitome Romanorum Pontificum" when commenting on the first sixty-nine popes on Malachy's list. This book was written in the reign of Pope Paul IV.

It is of interest to observe that the order of succession, particularly where the antipopes are concerned, has always been subject to editorial activity. I have started with the premise that the prophecies of Malachy concern the successors of St Peter in the Roman Catholic Church; the only legitimate order is therefore the one which is canonically correct. In the annual Vatican year book is a section: "Serie dei Sommi Pontefici Romani", which I have used with the kind permission of His Excellency the Apostolic Delegate to the United Kingdom. However, this has presented me with one problem: mention is made in the official list issued by the Vatican of an antipope INNOCENT III (di Sezze; Lando, 29.ix.1179-1180); this antipope does not appear in any of the commentaries of Malachy's prophecies. On the other hand, no mention is made in the official list of the antipope Clement VIII (1424-1429) whom, as I mentioned earlier, Panvinio ranks among the legitimate Popes of Rome. This is strange, and I have no explanation to offer. Among the 112 popes mentioned by Malachy are ten antipopes who all fall into the period between Alexander III (1159) and Nicolas V (1447). This alone makes the theory that the prophecies originated in the 16th century unlikely. References by previous interpreters concerning armorial bearings of popes before the latter part of the 12th century must be considered with caution because heraldic devices were not evident before that time. Papal armorial bearings, which we have reproduced from the same year book (Serie dei Sommi Pontefici) begin with the coat of arms of Pope Innocent III (1198-1216). The dates of election and accession to the See of St Peter are those officially recorded by the Vatican. Where there are more than one translation from Malachy's original Latin description, I have given those most commonly used in earlier commentaries.

NOTE

In my commentary on Malachy's prophecies I have made extensive use of the medieval interpretations and those of the 19th century. These, however, finish with *Crux de Cruce* (PIUS IX), and I have attempted to complete the interpretations up to *Flos Florum* (PAUL VI) on similar lines as those followed earlier.

For the reader's benefit I have added a brief "curriculum vitae" of the popes mentioned by Malachy. For references I have used I SOMMI PONTEFICI ROMANI (Vatican 1968) and THE CATHOLIC ENCYCLOPEDIA (New York). The papal coats of arms are reproduced from STEMMI DEI SOMMI PONTEFICI (Vatican 1968).

I wish to emphasize that my comments on the three prophecies yet to be fulfilled are pure guesses on my part and I beg the Dean and the College of Cardinals who will elect the future popes, not to be unduly influenced by my descriptions. I am sure that those eminent gentlemen whom my guess might fit, will forgive me for appearing to be canvassing. Finally, I wish to reiterate what I have said earlier, the final decision as to who is going to be the next pope and his successors, rests with the Holy Spirit.

P.B.

STEMMI DEI SOMMI PONTEFICI
DAL SEC. XII AD OGGI

INNOCENZO III	ONORIO III	GREGORIO IX	CELESTINO IV
1198 — 1216	1216 — 1227	1227 — 1241	1241 — 1241
LOTARIO DEI CONTI DI SEGNI	CENCIO SAVELLI	UGOLINO DEI CONTI DI SEGNI	GOFFREDO CASTIGLIONI
INNOCENZO IV	ALESSANDRO IV	URBANO IV	CLEMENTE IV
1243 — 1254	1254 — 1261	1261 — 1264	1265 — 1268
SINIBALDO FIESCHI	RINALDO DEI CONTI DI SEGNI	GIACOMO PANTALÉON	GUIDO FOULQUOIS
B. GREGORIO X	B. INNOCENZO V	ADRIANO V	GIOVANNI XXI
1271 — 1276	1276 — 1276	1276 — 1276	1276 — 1277
TEBALDO VISCONTI	PIETRO DI TARANTASIA	OTTOBONO FIESCHI	PIETRO IULIANI
NICCOLÒ III	MARTINO IV	ONORIO IV	NICCOLÒ IV
1277 — 1280	1281 — 1285	1285 — 1287	1288 — 1292
GIOVANNI GAETANO ORSINI	SIMONE DE BRION	GIACOMO SAVELLI	GIROLAMO MASCI

17

EX CASTRO TIBERIS
From a Castle on the Tiber

CELESTINE II
1143 - 1144

GUIDO DE CASTELLO

Guido de Castello was a native of Roman Tuscany whose date of birth is unknown. He died on the 8th March 1144. He was made Cardinal in 1128, in 1140 he was made Papal Legate to France where he incurred the displeasure of St Bernard for the protection accorded by him to Arnold of Brescia. He succeeded Innocent II on the 25th September 1143 and at once lifted from France the interdict that his predecessor had inflicted because of the act of Louis VII in opposing his own candidate to the rightfully elected Bishop of Bourges. On the eve of a serious conflict with Roger of Sicily, Celestine II died, after a short reign of about six months.

Malachy's prophecy is a reference to the Pope's family name.

INIMICUS EXPULSUS
The enemy expelled

LUCIUS II
1144 - 1145

GERARDO CACCIANEMICI

Gerardo was born in Bologna (date unknown) and he died in Rome on the 15th February 1145. Before entering the Roman Curia he was a Canon in Bologna. In 1124 he was created Cardinal Priest and from 1125 to 1126 he was Papal Legate in Germany. During the pontificate of Innocent II we find Gerardo three times as Legate in Germany, and it was largely due to him that King Lothiar III made two expeditions to Italy for the purpose of protecting Innocent II against the antipope Anacletus II. Towards the end of the pontificate of Innocent II he was appointed Papal Counsellor and Librarian. On the 12th March 1144 he was elected and consecrated Pope. His reign was a troubled one and if we can believe the statement of Godfrey de Viterbo in his *Pantheon,* Lucius II marched upon the Capitol at the head of a small army where he suffered defeat and was severely injured by stones that were thrown upon him on this occasion and which caused his death a few days later. During his reign he was especially well disposed towards the order of the Premonstratensians.

Malachy's description *Inimicus expulsus* appears to be an allusion to the Pope's family name. We have already stated what his family name was; *Cacciare* in Italian means to expel and *nemici* are the enemies.

EX MAGNITUDINE MONTIS
From the great mountain

EUGENE III
1145 - 1153

BERNARDO FORSE DEI PAGANELLI DI MONTEMAGNO

Bernardo was elected Pope on the 15th February 1145, and died in Tivoli on the 8th July 1153. On the same day that Pope Lucius died, the Sacred College foreseeing that the Roman populace would make a determined effort to force the new Pope to abdicate his temporal power, withdrew to the remote cloisters of St Caesarius and elected a candidate outside their body. They chose, unanimously, the Cistercian monk Bernard of Pisa, Abbot of the monastery of Tre

Fontane. He was enthroned as Eugene III without delay, and since residence in the rebellious city was impossible, the Pope and his Cardinals fled to the country. St Bernard received the news of the elevation of his disciple with astonishment and pleasure and wrote to the new Pope a letter containing the famous and often quoted passage — "Who will grant me to see, before I die, the Church of God as in the days of old, when the apostles laid down their nets for a draught, not of silver and gold, but of souls?" Eugene is said to have gained the affection of the people by his affability and generosity. During his lifetime he continued to wear the coarse habit of Clairveaux beneath the purple and the virtues monasticism accompanied him through his stormy career. St Antoninus described Eugene III as one of the greatest and most afflicted Popes.

Malachy's *ex magnitudine montis* refers to his place of birth, Montemagno.

ABBAS SUBURRANUS
Abbot from Suburra

ANASTASIUS IV
1153 - 1154

CORRADO

Corrado was crowned Pope on the 12th July 1153 and died in Rome on the 3rd December of the following year. He is chiefly known for his attitude towards Frederick Barbarossa and his recognition of Wichmann as Bishop of Magdeburg. Interpreters of Malachy differ in their explanation of the word *Suburranus*. Some refer to his birth-place, which is said to have been a locality called *Suburra,* others maintain that *Suburranus* is used in reference to one steering a great vessel.

DE RURE ALBO

(a) From a white country

(b) Of the Alban country

ADRIAN IV
1154 - 1159

NICHOLAS BREAKSPEAR

Little is known about the parentage or boyhood of Adrian although it is recorded that he was probably born in Abbots Langley, Hertfordshire. Adrian went abroad as a poor wandering scholar and begged his way to the famous university of Paris. He was admitted among the regular canons of St Rufus, where he was successively raised to the office of Prior and Abbot. However, the canons repented of their choice and appealed to the Pope on two occasions, bringing various charges against him. Pope Eugene ordered the canons to elect another Abbot and raised Adrian to the rank of Cardinal Bishop of Albano in 1146. He was sent as Papal Legate to the kingdoms of Denmark, Sweden and Norway. On his return to Rome he was hailed the Apostle of the North and as the death of Anastasius IV occurred at that time on 2nd December 1154, Adrian was unanimously elected the successor of St Peter on the following day. The turbulent and fickle population of Rome was once again in open revolt under the leadership of Arnold of Brescia. King William of Sicily also showed open hostility and the professed friendship of Frederick Barbarossa was even more dangerous. When Cardinal Gerardo was mortally wounded in broad daylight, Adrian at once laid the city under an interdict and retired to Viterbo. He forbade the observance of any sacred service until the Wednesday of Holy Week and the Senators were impelled to prostrate themselves before His Holiness. Submission was made and the ban removed. In June 1155 the famous meeting between Frederick of Hohenstauffen, then the most powerful ruler in Europe, and Adrian, the most powerful spiritual leader in the world, took place about thirty miles north of Rome. This ultimately led to the crowning of Frederick in St Peter's. In 1156 Adrian collected his vassals and mercenaries and marched south to Beneventum where he remained until June 1156. It was during this time that John of Salisbury spent three months with him and obtained from the Pope the famous Donation of Ireland. In his work *Metalogicus* John records, "At my solicitation (ad preces meas) he (Adrian IV) granted Ireland to Henry II, the illustrious King of England, to hold by hereditary right, as his letter to this day testifies. For all Ireland of ancient right, according to the Donation of Constantine, was said to belong to the Roman Church which he founded. He also sent by me a ring of gold, with the best of emeralds therein, wherewith the investiture might be made for his governorship of Ireland, and that same ring was ordered to be and is still in the public treasury of the king."

The suggestion that because he was born in England Adrian made Ireland over to King Henry II, who was no relation of his, does not merit serious attention. The only objection raised to John of Salisbury's statement is that it may be an interpolation. If it is not an interpolation it constitutes a complete proof of the donation, the investiture by the ring being legally sufficient. The Pope's Bull known as *Laudabiliter* does not purport to confer Ireland by hereditary right, but the letter referred to was not the Bull but a formal letter of investiture. The overwhelming weight of authority is in favour of the genuineness of the passage in *Metalogicus*. The Bull *Laudabiliter* has often been considered doubtful. Assuming the statements in *Metalogicus* to be correct, the text relating to the donation of Adrian may be arranged as follows: —

(1) The letter of investiture referred to by John of Salisbury, 1156.

(2) *Laudabiliter*, prepared in 1156 and issued in 1159,

(3) A confirmation of the letter of investiture by Alexander III in 1159.

(4) Three letters of Alexander III in 1172 which confirm *Laudabiliter*.

The Bull was not sent forward in 1156, because the offer of Adrian was not then acted on, but the investiture was accepted. At a council held in Winchester on the 29th September 1156 the question of subduing Ireland and giving it to William, Henry's brother, was considered, but the expedition was put off to another time.

The donation of Adrian was subsequently recognised in many official writings, and the Pope, for more than four centuries, claimed the overlordship of Ireland.

Pope Adrian IV died at Anagni in open strife with the Emperor Frederick Barbarossa who was in league with the Lombards against him. Alexander III carried out the intentions of Adrian and shortly afterwards excommunicated the Emperor.

Malachy's prophecy *de rure albo* appears to be most appropriate. Adrian was born in England, which was called Albion on account of the white rocks and white cliffs. His birthplace was near the Abbey of St Albans and he was consecrated Cardinal Bishop of Albano. Last, but not least, he was hailed the Apostle of the North, where he had worked in countries of perpetual snow.

EX ANSERE CUSTODE
From the guardian goose

ALEXANDER III
1159 - 1181

ROLANDO BANDINELLI

Rolando Bandinelli was born of a distinguished Sienese family. He was a professor in Bologna and was called to Rome by Eugene III in the year 1150, where he soon became Cardinal of the title of St Mark and Papal Counsellor. After the death of Pope Adrian IV (1st September 1159), of the twenty-two Cardinals assembled to elect a successor all but three voted for Rolando. In opposition to Cardinal Rolando, who took the name of Alexander III, the three imperialist members of the conclave chose one of their own number, Cardinal Octavian, who assumed the title of Victor IV. The Emperor summoned both claimants before a packed assembly at Pavia where he addressed Octavian as Victor IV, and the canonically elected Pope as Cardinal Rolando. Pope Alexander refused to submit his clear right to this tribunal, which, as was foreseen, declared for the usurper on the 11th February 1160. Alexander promptly responded by excommunicating the Emperor and releasing his subjects from their oaths of allegiance. The ensuing schism was far more disastrous to the empire than to the papacy. It lasted for seventeen years and only ended after the battle of Legnano in 1176, with the unconditional surrender of Barbarossa, in Venice, in 1177. Alexander's enforced exile in France 1162 to 1165) helped greatly to enhance the dignity of the papacy, never so popular as when in distress. It also brought him into direct contact with the most powerful monarch of the West, Henry II of England. After Thomas Becket's murder the Pope succeeded, without actual recourse to ban or interdict, in obtaining from the penitent monarch every right for which the martyr had died.

In 1179 Alexander convoked and presided over the third Lateran Council. At this council the exclusive right of papal elections was vested in a two-third majority of the Cardinals. Alexander III died on the 3rd August 1181.

Panvinio refers to Alexander as *de familia Paparona*. In Ciacconius' edition (1677) it is stated that he belonged to the noble family of "Bandinella" which was afterwards called Paparona. Referring to the Pope's family coat of arms, Ciacconius maintains that there was a goose in it. Another interpreter reminds the reader that the family of Alexander III descended from one of those who, aroused by geese, when Brennus attempted to sack the capital, repulsed him. In this particular case the entire evidence for Malachy appears to rest on the assumption that the family name of the Pope was Paparona. There seems to be an absolute definiteness about this in early interpretations. Panvinio, who is usually relied upon whenever a question of genealogy is raised, finds himself criticised by later interpreters for "chiming in with the prophecy". Abbé Cucherat explains the legend by a classic allusion to the honoured bird which saved Rome. According to him Malachy made a classic, as well as mystic, allusion to the salvation of Rome by Alexander III.

EX TETRO CARCERE
From the Loathsome Prison

V I C T O R I V (ANTIPOPE)
1159 - 1164

OTTAVIANO MONTICELLO

Ottaviano was Cardinal of the title of St Nicholas at the Tullian prison. Panvinio gives him the same title, whilst others proclaim him to be Cardinal of St Sicilia. He was elected on the 7th September 1159 by a small minority of Cardinals, the clergy of St Peter and the Roman populace, while the majority of the College of Cardinals elected Cardinal Rolando who assumed the title of Alexander III. Ottaviano belonged to one of the most powerful Roman families (Count Tuscalan's) and had been a Cardinal since 1138. As he was considered a great friend of Barbarossa he rested his hopes on the Emperor backing his election to the Papal see. He died at Lucca on the 20th April 1164 and was succeeded by the antipope Paschal III.

Malachy's Latin description is an allusion to his Cardinal title.

VIA TRANSTIBERINA
The road beyond the Tiber

P A S C H A L I I I (ANTIPOPE)
1164 - 1168

GUIDO DA CREMA

Via Transtiberina refers to St Mary's in Transtevere, which was the Cardinal title of Paschal III. He was elected in 1164 to succeed Cardinal Ottaviano. To meet the demands of Frederick Barbarossa he canonized Charlemagne in 1165, but this action was never ratified by the Church. He died in 1168. There appears to be a great confusion among interpreters of Malachy, because the said cardinal title is often given to the antipope Callixtus III. According to Ciacconius, Paschal III and Callixtus III, together with their dates, should change places, and the rest should be left to stand. Others maintain that Callixtus had no title in the city of Rome. So that the reader may be aware of this confusion I prefer to introduce the next antipope, Callixtus III, at this point, rather than be guilty of presenting an authoritative statement as to their respective Cardinal titles.

DE PANNONIA TUSCIÆ
From the Hungary of Tuscia

C A L L I X T U S   I I I
1168 - 29/8/1178*

GIOVANNI DI STRUMI

Callixtus III was the Hungarian John, Abbot of Struma.

Malachy's Latin legend for Paschal III and Callixtus III are obvious allusions to their ecclesiastical titles, which appear to be in dispute. However, historians are satisfied that Paschal was in fact Cardinal Bishop of St Mary in Transtevere and Callixtus was from Hungary.

At this point the *Serie dei Sommi Pontefici Romani* gives yet another antipope, Innocent III. His place of origin is Sezze, Lando, and his tenure of office is given as 1179 to 1180. There is no reference to Innocent III (the antipope) in Malachy or any of his interpreters. [See Clement VIII].

---

* date of his submission to Alexander III.

LUX IN OSTIO
(a) The light at the door.
(b) The light in Ostium
(c) A light in the gate

LUCIUS III

1181 - 1185

Ubaldo Allucingoli

Ubaldo was born in Lucca and created Cardinal Priest in 1141. In 1159 he became Cardinal Bishop of Ostia. After the death of Alexander III he was elected Pope in Velletri where he was crowned. He was compelled to leave Rome in 1182, but returned the following year in an attempt to put an end to the continual dissensions of the Romans. However, his life was made so unbearable that he had to leave the city for a second time. Though the relations between Lucius III and the Emperor Frederick I were not openly hostile they were always strained. Lucius III did not yield to the Emperor and demanded that German Bishops, unlawfully appointed by the anti-popes during the pontificate of Alexander III, should be re-consecrated and retain their sees. He died at Verona on the 25th November 1185.

Malachy's description appears to be a play on the words Lucius or Lucca and Ostia.

SUS IN CRIBRO
A sow in a sieve

URBAN III

1185 - 1187

Uberto of the noble milanese family of Crivelli

Uberto was created a Cardinal by Lucius III in 1182 and Archbishop of Milan in 1185. He was elected to succeed Lucius and crowned on 1st December 1185. Urban inherited from his predecessor a legacy of feud with the great Emperor Frederick Barbarossa and this was embittered by personal hostility, for at the sack of Milan in 1162 the Emperor had caused several of the Pope's relatives to be mutilated. He died at Ferrara on the 19th October 1187.

Malachy's description is an allusion to the Pope's family name, Crivelli: Crivelli in Italian means a sieve. In his *Epitome*, Panvinio gives the arms of the Pope and there is a distinct representation of a sieve on the shield and the supporters of the crest are two sows. Ciacconius only gives the sieve.

ENSIS LAURENTII
The sword of Lawrence

GREGORY VIII
1187

Alberto de Morra

This Pope had only a pontificate of one month and 27 days. The year 1187 witnessed the almost complete obliteration of Christianity in Palestine. The fall of the Holy City struck Europe and Urban III is said to have died of a broken heart on 20th October. The following day the Cardinals elected Cardinal Alberto, a Beneventan of noble family. He was created Cardinal in 1155 and given the title of San Lorenzo in Lucina in 1158. He died in Pisa on the 17th December 1187.

There are two possible allusions in the prophecies of Malachy: firstly, Gregory VIII had been Cardinal of St Lawrence, and secondly, his armorial bearing was a drawn sword.

DE SCHOLA EXIET
- (a)   He shall go forth from the school
- (b)   He will come out of a school
- (c)   Departed from school

CLEMENT III
1187 - 1191

PAOLO SCOLARI

During the short space (1181-1188) which separated the pontificates of Alexander III and Innocent III, not less than five pontiffs occupied the Papal chair in swift succession. They were all veterans trained in the school of Alexander. Two days after Gregory VIII's death the Cardinal Bishop of Palestrina, Paolo Scolari, was elected to the See of St Peter. This was a popular choice for the Romans, because he was the first Roman to be thus elevated to the papacy since the rebellion in the days of Arnold of Brescia. From the beginning, Pope Clement III concentrated on the task of massing the forces of Christendom against the· Saracens. He was the organiser of the Third Crusade. His death occurred on the 27th March 1191.

Malachy's legend is merely an allusion to his family name and is to be understood as foretelling that this Pope was to be one of the Scolari.

DE (EX) RURE BOVENSI
- (a)   From the Bovensian Territory
- (b)   From the cattle country
- (c)   From the country of Bovis

CELESTINE III
1191 - 1198

GIACINTO BOBONE

Giacinto Bobone was born in 1106 and became the first of the Roman family of Orsini to ascend to the chair of St Peter. On 30th

March 1191, in his eighty-fifth year, he was elected to succeed Clement III after forty-seven years as a Cardinal. As he was only a Cardinal Deacon, he was ordained Priest on the 13th April, and consecrated Bishop the next day. The following day he anointed and crowned King Henry VI of Germany as Emperor. Pope Celestine III canonized St Malachy of Armagh.

Malachy's description refers once again to the Pope's family name.

COMES SIGNATUS
A signed Count (Conti-Segni)

INNOCENT III
1198 - 1216

LOTARIO DEI CONTI DI SEGNI

Lotario was born in 1160 in Anagni, the son of Count Trasimund of Segni and a nephew of Clement III. He became an outstanding theologian and when he returned to Rome after the death of Alexander III he held various ecclesiastical offices during the reigns of successive popes. Pope Gregory VIII created him Cardinal Deacon of St George in 1190 and later Cardinal Priest. During the pontificate of Celestine III, who was a member of the Houses of Orsini, enemies of the Counts of Segni, he lived in retirement. After the Pope's death Lotario was elected Pope on the same day on which Celestine III died. He was only 37 years old. There was scarcely a country in Europe over which Innocent III did not in some way or other assert the supremacy which he claimed for the papacy. He was a zealous protector of the true faith and a strenuous opponent of heresy. His great political/ecclesiastical achievements brought the papacy to the zenith of its power. He died on the 16th June 1216 in Perugia.

Malachy's legend refers to the illustrious family of the Conti of which the Conti di Segni was a branch.

CANONICUS DE LATERE
(a)　A Canon from the side
(b)　Canon of Lateran

HONORIUS III

1216 - 1227

CENCIO SAVELLI

Cencio Savelli was born in Rome and was for a time canon at the Church of Santa Maria Maggiore. He became Papal Chamberlain in 1188 and Cardinal Deacon of Santa Lucia in 1193. Under Pope Innocent III he became Cardinal Priest of St John and St Paul and was appointed tutor to the future Emperor Frederick II in 1197. On the 18th July 1216, nineteen cardinals assembled in Perugia, where Innocent had died two days previously. The Cardinals agreed to an election by compromise and Cardinal Ugolino of Ostia (afterwards Pope Gregory IX) and Cardinal Guido of Praeneste were empowered to appoint a new Pope. Cencio Savelli was chosen and consecrated in Perugia and crowned in Rome on the 31st August. Again this was a popular choice in Rome. Unlike his predecessor he was very advanced in age when acceding to the papal throne. Honorius III became the patron of three great orders. He approved the rule of St Dominic in his Bull *Religiosam Vitam* on the 22nd December 1216, and that of St Francis in his Bull *Solet Annuere* on the 29th November 1223. On the 13th January 1226 he approved the Carmelite order in his Bull *Ut Vivendi Normam*. It is remarkable that out of six saints who were canonized by Honorius III, four were English or Irish. He died at Rome on the 18th March 1227.

Malachy obviously refers to the fact that Cencio Savelli was a canon of St John Lateran.

AVIS OSTIENSIS
The Bird of Ostia

G R E G O R Y   I X
1227 - 1241

Ugolino, dei Conti di Segni

Ugolino was born in 1145 at Anagni. Educated at Paris and Bologna and appointed successively Papal Chaplain, Archpriest of St Peter and Cardinal Deacon in 1198. In May 1206 he succeeded Octavian as Cardinal Bishop of Ostia. Honorius III made him Plenipotentiary Legate in 1217 and on the 18th March 1227, after the death of Pope Honorius III, the Cardinals once again agreed upon an election by compromise. Two of the three Cardinal electors were Ugolino and Conrad of Urach. At first Conrad of Urach was elected, but he refused the tiara lest it might appear that he had elected himself. All the Cardinals unanimously elected Ugolino on the 19th March 1227. He was then more than eighty years old. When still Cardinal Bishop of Ostia, Gregory IX would often wear the dress of St Francis, walk about barefoot with him and his disciples and discuss theological matters with Francis. St Francis loved him as his father, and in a prophetic spirit used to address him as "the Bishop of the whole world and the father of all nations". He was also a devoted friend of St Dominic and promoted the interests of his order in many ways. St Clare and her order stood also under the protection of Gregory IX. He was a great patron of other religious orders with whose help he planned the conversion of Asia and Africa. For a time Gregory IX lived in hope that he might bring about a reunion of the Latin and Greek Churches. In 1232 the Patriarch of Constantinople acknowledged the Papal primacy, but Gregory failed, like many other popes before and after him, in his efforts to reunite the two churches.

During the 13 years of his pontificate he created fourteen Cardinals, many of whom were members of religious orders. He died on the 22nd August 1241 at Rome. The arms of Gregory IX show an eagle and he was Cardinal Bishop of Ostia. This is the first allusion to armorial bearings which can now be used in evidence. [See *Stemmi dei Sommi Pontefici*].

LEO SABINUS
The Sabinian Lion

CELESTINE IV
1241

GOFFREDO CASTIGLIONI

This pope was a native of Milan and a nephew of Urban III. He was probably a Cistercian. He was made a Cardinal by Gregory IX and succeeded him on the 25th October 1241. His death occurred after a reign of only fifteen days.

Malachy's prophecy is an allusion to the Pope's armorial bearing which features a lion. He is also said to have been Cardinal Bishop of Sabina (Episcopus Cardinalis Satinus) which, of course, has nothing to do with the Church and Convent of Saint Sabina in Rome.

COMES LAURENTIUS
Count Laurence

INNOCENT IV
1243 - 1254

SINIBALDO FIESCHI (COUNT OF LAVAGNA)

Born of one of the noble families of Genoa, Fieschi became Cardinal Priest of St Laurence in Lucina in 1228. When Celestine IV had died, the excommunicated Emperor Frederick II was in possession of the states of the Church around Rome and attempted to intimidate the Cardinals into electing a Pope of his choice. The Cardinals fled to Anagni and voted for Sinibaldo Fieschi, who ascended the Papal throne as Innocent IV in June 1243, after an interregnum of one year, seven months and fifteen days.

Sinibaldo Fieschi was Cardinal of St Laurence and Malachy's prophecy is an obvious reference to this.

SIGNUM OSTIENSE
(a)   A sign of Ostia
(b)   The standard of Ostia

ALEXANDER IV
1254 - 1261

RINALDO DEI SIGNORI DI IENNE

Rinaldo was born of the noble house of Segni which had already given two sons to the Papacy, and was created Cardinal Bishop of Ostia by his uncle Gregory IX. On the death of Innocent IV in 1254, the aged Cardinal was unanimously chosen to succeed him. As Pope he showed great favour to the Order of St Francis and one of his first acts was to canonise St Clare. He died on the 25th May 1261.

Signum Ostiense is an enigmatic way of pointing to the Bishop being of the house of Conti-Segni and also Cardinal Bishop of Ostia.

HIERUSALEM CAMPANIÆ
Jerusalem of Champagne

URBAN IV
1261 - 1264

JACQUES PANTALEON

Jacques, the son of a French cobbler, was born in Troyes. After being a Canon and Archdeacon of Liège, he became Bishop of Verdun in 1254 and Patriarch of Jerusalem in 1255. After the death of Alexander IV he was elected Pope. He died on the 2nd October 1264.

Born in Champagne and raised to the title of Patriarch of Jerusalem, Malachy's description appears most appropriate.

DRACO DEPRESSUS
The dragon crushed

CLEMENT IV
1265 - 1268

Guido Fulcodi

Guido was born in Saint-Gilles on the Rhone, and made a rapid rise in the Church. In 1261 he became Cardinal Bishop of Sabina and was elected Pope, against his will, on the 5th February 1265. He accepted this position with great reluctance. After his death in 1268 the Papal throne remained vacant for nearly three years.

Panvinio in his *Epitome* shows an eagle clawing a dragon. However, his official coat of arms shows six fleurs de lis. Abbé Cucherat explains the Latin Legend metaphorically by pointing out that Pope Clement IV crushed nepotism, which he describes as the dragon in the Church at that time. It is a well documented fact that his first act as Pope was to forbid any of his relatives to come to the Curia, or to attempt to derive any sort of temporai advantage from his elevation.

ANGUINEUS VIR
(a)   The man of the serpent
(b)   A snake-like man

GREGORY X
1271 - 1276

Tebaldo Visconti

Tebaldo Visconti was born in 1210 and became Archdeacon of Liège. After the death of Pope Clement IV the French and Italian Cardinals could not agree on a candidate. Three years later they voted for Tedaldo Visconti, who was not only not a Cardinal but not even a priest. He accepted the Papal dignity and took the name of Gregory X. From the very beginning of his pontificate Gregory sought to promote the interests of the Holy Land. He died on the 10th January 1276.

Again the coat of arms as given by Panvinio differs substantially from that which is attributed to him in later centuries. Panvinio quite plainly shows a serpent in the armorial bearings of the Pope and his family.

CONCIONATOR GALLUS
A French Preacher

INNOCENT V
1276

Petrus A Tarantasia

Born in 1225 in south eastern France, Tarantasia became Archbishop of Lyons in 1272 and Cardinal Bishop of Ostia in 1273. He was the intimate adviser of Gregory X whom he succeeded on the 21st January 1276. Thus he became the first Dominican Pope. He died in June 1276.

Malachy's prophecy refers to Innocent V having been a member of the order of Preachers, and a Frenchman.

BONUS COMES
A Good Count

ADRIAN V
1276

Ottobono Fieschi

This nephew of Innocent IV reigned only from the 12th July to the 21st August 1276. Adrian V was a count and his name Ottobono furnishes an explanation to the second half of the prophecy.

PISCATOR TUSCUS
A Tuscan Fisherman

J O H N   X X I
1276 - 1277*

PIETRO JULIANI

Pietro was born in Lisbon. He was appointed Cardinal Bishop of Tusculum and in 1276 he was elected to succeed Adrian V. On the 14th May 1277 while the Pope was alone in his apartment, it collapsed and he was buried under the ruins.

Piscator obviously refers to his name Petrus; Tuscus is an adjective used (probably in error) to refer to Tusculum.

ROSA COMPOSITA
(a)   The Modest Rose   (b)   The Rose Composite

N I C H O L A S   I I I
1277 - 1280

GIOVANNI GAETANO ORSINI

Giovanni was born in Rome in 1216 of the the illustrious Roman family of Orsini. He was created Cardinal Deacon with a title of St Nicholas by Innocent IV. After the death of John XXI he succeeded him as Pope in 1277.

Giovanni Gaetano Orsini bore a rose in his coat of arms.

---

* After John XIV had been removed by force, the usurper Boniface VII reigned eleven months, dying in July 985. A Roman named John was then elected Pope and crowned. Some historians, and even Papal catalogues, give as the immmediate successor to Boniface yet another John, who is supposed to have reigned for four months and is placed by a few historians in the list of Popes as John XV. Although this alleged Pope John never existed, the fact that he has been catalogued by these historians has trown into disorder the enumeration of the Popes named John, the true John XV often being called John XVI. This confusion was remedied when Cardinal Roncalli took the name John XXIII, ascending to the throne of St Peter in 1958, nearly 1,000 years after the confusion started.

EX TELONIO LILIACEI MARTINI

(a)   From the office of Martin of the lilies

(b)   From the receipt of custom of Martin of the lilies

MARTIN IV

1281 - 1285

SIMONE DE BRION

Simone was born in the Castle of Montpensier in the old French province of Touraine, and became Canon and Treasurer at the Church of St Martin in Tours. King Louis IX made him Chancellor of France in 1260 and Urban VI created him a Cardinal. Six months after the death of Pope Nicholas III, Simone de Brion was unanimously elected Pope in 1281. He died on the 28th March 1285.

St Malachy obviously refers to the Pope's position as Treasurer of St Martin of Tours; the fleur-de-lis is a well known emblem of France.

EX ROSA LEONINA

From the leonine Rose

HONORIUS IV

1285 - 1287

GIACOMO SAVELLI

Giacomo Savelli, who was born in Rome in 1210 had, it seems, an unspectacular career before ascending to the Papal throne. In 1261 he was created Cardinal by Martin IV who also made him Captain of the Papal army. His election to the papacy was one of the speediest in history; three days after the death of Pope Martin IV fifteen out of the eighteen Cardinals who then composed the Sacred College elected the Pope without the Conclave, which had been prescribed by Gregory X, but suspended by John XXI. At the first vote taken Giacomo Savelli was unanimously elected and took the name of Honorius IV. He died in Rome on the 3rd April 1287.

Malachy's description is an allusion to the Pope's coat of arms which shows two lions holding a rose.

PICUS INTER ESCAS
A woodpecker among the food

NICHOLAS IV
1288 - 1292

GIROLAMO MASCI

Pope Nicholas IV had entered the Franciscan order at an early age and was sent in 1272 as a delegate to Constantinople to invite the participation of the Greeks in the Second Council of Lyons. Two years later he succeeded St Bonaventure in the Generalship of his order. He was created a Cardinal in 1278 and Martin IV appointed him Bishop of Palestrina. After the death of Honorius IV on the 3rd April 1278 the Conclave was hopelessly divided in its election of a successor. It was not until the following year on the 15th February 1288 that the Cardinal unanimously elected Girolamo Masci. He died in Rome on the 4th April 1292.

Malachy's prophecy is most obscure. It has been suggested that *Picus inter escas* is an enigmatic allusion to the fact that Nicholas came from Ascoli in Picenum; however, this explanation appears to me to be too far fetched. On the other hand I have no better one to offer, as the records of the Pope's life are very sketchy.

The fact that Malachy's description makes little sense to us does not prove that it was meaningless at the time when it was made or when Nicholas IV became Pope.

S. CELESTINO V	BONIFACIO VIII	B. BENEDETTO XI	CLEMENTE V
1294 — 1294	1294 — 1303	1303 — 1304	1305 — 1314
PIETRO DEL MURRONE	BENEDETTO CAETANI	NICCOLÒ BOCCASINI	BERTRANDO DE GOT
GIOVANNI XXII	BENEDETTO XII	CLEMENTE VI	INNOCENZO VI
1316 — 1334	1334 — 1342	1342 — 1352	1352 — 1362
GIACOMO DUÈSE	GIACOMO FOURNIER	PIETRO ROGER	STEFANO AUBERT
B. URBANO V	GREGORIO XI	URBANO VI	BONIFACIO IX
1362 — 1370	1370 — 1378	1378 — 1389	1389 — 1404
GUGLIELMO DE GRIMOARD	PIETRO ROGER DE BEAUFORT	BARTOLOMEO PRIGNANO	PIETRO TOMACELLI
INNOCENZO VII	GREGORIO XII	CLEMENTE VII	BENEDETTO XIII
1404 — 1406	1406 — 1415	1378 antip. 1394	1394 antip. 1423
COSMA MIGLIORATI	ANGELO CORRER	ROBERTO DEI CONTI DEL GENEVOIS	PIETRO DE LUNA
ALESSANDRO V	GIOVANNI XXIII	MARTINO V	EUGENIO IV
1409 antip. 1410	1410 antip. 1415	1417 — 1431	1431 — 1447
PIETRO FILARGO	BALDASSARRE COSSA	ODDONE COLONNA	GABRIELE CONDULMER

EX EREMO CELSUS

(a)   Elevated from the desert
(b)   The lofty one from the desert

C E L E S T I N E   V

1294

Pietro di Murrone

Pietro was born in 1215, and became a Benedictine at the age of 17. His love of solitude led hi minto the wilderness of Montemorrone and later into the wilderness of Mount Majella. He followed the example of John the Baptist and wore hair-cloth roughened with knots. A chain of iron was fastened around him every day except Sundays, and for long stretches of time he lived on bread and water. In July 1294 three Cardinals accompanied by a great multitude of monks ascended the mountain and announced that Pietro had been chosen Pope by a unanimous vote of the Sacred College. Two years and three months had elapsed since the death of Nicholas IV. Pietro heard of his elevation with tears, but after a brief prayer obeyed what seemed the clear voice of God. Owing to his inexperience of diplomatic matters the affairs of the Curia fell into extreme disorder and he looked upon affairs of state as wasting time that ought to be devoted to exercises of piety. Because he feared that his soul was in danger he proposed abdication. The question arose for the first time whether a Pope could resign. On the 13th December he summoned the Cardinals and announced his resignation and proclaimed the Cardinals free to proceed to a new election. He was most cruelly treated by his successor Boniface VIII, who had him arrested and imprisoned. He died in prison on 19th May 1296.

Malachy's prophecy appears to have been remarkably fulfilled.

EX UNDARUM BENEDICTIONE
From a blessing of the waves

BONIFACE VIII

1294 - 1303

BENEDETTO CAETANI

Born in 1235 in Rome, Benedetto was the son of a noble Spanish family which had established itself in Gaeta and later in Anagni. Through his mother he was related to the house of Segni. He obtained a doctorate in Canon and Civil Law and in 1265 he accompanied Cardinal Fieschi to England to restore harmony between Henry III and the rebellious barons. In 1276 he entered upon his career in the Curia where he soon acquired considerable influence. The abdication of Pope Celestine V has been frequently ascribed to the undue influence and pressure of Cardinal Caetani. It is probable that the elevation of this simple minded and inexperienced recluse did not commend itself to a man like Caetani, reputed to be the greatest jurist of his age and well skilled in the arts of Curial diplomacy. There can be no question that he treated his predecessor most cruelly. He entertained the most exalted notions on the subject of papal supremacy and was most emphatic in the assertion of his claims. His reign was marked by political intrigues all over the Western world in which he played no mean part. Reports that he died in a frenzy, gnawing his hands and beating his brains out against a wall, have never been proved. He died in Rome on the 11th October 1303.

The Latin legend of Malachy has been interpreted as referring to the Pope's armorial bearing, combined with the reference to his Christian name.

CONCIONATOR PATAREUS
A preacher from Patara

BENEDICT XI
1303 - 1304

NICHOLAS BOCCASINI

Nicholas was born in 1240 and entered the Dominican order at the age of fourteen. In 1296 he was elected Master General of the order. In this position he became one of the defenders of the unpopular Pontiff, who showed him many marks of favour and confidence. He became Bishop of Ostia and Dean of the Sacred College and when in 1303 the enemies of the Pope had made themselves masters of the Sacred Palace, only he and another Cardinal remained at the side of Boniface VIII to defend him. In October that year he was unanimously elected Pope. After a brief pontificate of eight months Benedict XI died suddenly. It was suspected that he had been poisoned.

Nicholas was a native of Patara and belonged to the Order of Preachers.

DE FESSIS AQUITANICIS
(a) From the ditches of Aquitaine
(b) From the Aquitanian fesses

CLEMENT V
1305 - 1314

BERTRAND DE GOT

Bertrand de Got was born in France in 1264, of a distinguished family, his elder brother being the Archbishop of Lyons. He himself became Archbishop of Bordeaux. In 1305 after a Conclave of eleven months Bertrand de Got was elected Pope. During the usual Papal procession the Pope was thrown from his horse by a falling wall; one of his brothers was killed and so was Cardinal Matteo Orsini who had taken part in twelve Conclaves and seen thirteen Popes. The most precious jewel in the Papal crown was lost that day, an incident which has been prophetically interpreted by many. He died in April 1314.

Malachy's prophecy refers to the fact that the Pope came from Aquitania and makes heraldic reference to his armorial bearings.

DE SUTORE OSSEO
From the shoemaker of Osse

JOHN XXII
1316 - 1334

JACQUES DUESE

Jacques was born in 1249 and received his early education from the Dominicans. He became Bishop of Frejus in 1300 and Cardinal in 1312. After the death of Clement V the Papal See was vacant for two years and four months. In 1316 Jacques was chosen Pope. After his coronation at Lyons, John XXII moved to Avignon where he fixed his residence. He died on the 4th December 1334. His financial measures and centralisation of administration, and the fact that the transfer of the Papacy from Rome to Avignon had been made in the interests of France, made the Curia of Avignon generally detested. In fact the widespread distrust of the Papacy could not fail to result in consequences detrimental to the interior life of the Church.

Historians have always maintained that Jacques Duèse was the son of a shoemaker named Osse. If this is so, the legend is perfectly clear.

CORVUS SCHISMATICUS
A schismatical crow

NICHOLAS V (ANTIPOPE)
1328 - 1330

PIETRO RAINALLUCCI

In 1328 the excommunicated German King Louis of Bavaria received in Rome the Imperial Crown from Sciarra Colonna and on April 18th, and in the name of Louis of Bavaria, proclaimed John XXII a heretic, usurper and oppressor of the Church and also deprived him of his Papal dignities. A straw image of the Pope was publically burned in Rome and on the 12th May a Franciscan monk Pietro was proclaimed antipope by Louis, taking at his consecration the name of Nicholas V. In August 1330 Pietro wrote to Pope John XXII asking for pardon and absolution. This was granted; but Pietro was never allowed to leave the city where he spent the three remaining years of his life in voluntary penance and study. He died in 1333.

Medieval interpreters give this pope's name as Peter de Corberia or de Corbavio; the Vatican calender lists him as Pietro Rainallucci di Corvaro. Corvus appears an obvious allusion to the Pope's place of origin and, Schismaticus places him among the ranks of the antipopes.

FRIGIDUS ABBAS
The cold Abbot

BENEDICT XII
1334 - 1342

JACQUES FOURNIER

Jacques was a Cistercian monk in the Monastery of Fontforide. The Abbot there was his uncle, Arnold Novelli, by whose name

Fournier was also known. He later became Abbot himself and was created Cardinal in 1310. He received the necessary two-thirds vote in December 1334 and was enthroned as Benedict XII on the 8th January 1335. He encounted much criticism and resentment and he died in Avignon in 1342.

Malachy's legend is explained by Panvinio's description "Abbas monasterii Fontis Frigidi".

EX ROSA ATRABENSIS
From the Rose of Arras

CLEMENT VI

1342 - 1352

PIERRE ROGER

Pierre Roger was born in 1291 in France and entered a Benedictine Monastery at the age of ten. He rapidly rose from one ecclesiastical dignity to another and he became Bishop of Arras and Chancellor of France in 1328. He was created a Cardinal in 1338 by Benedict XII whom he succeeded as Pontiff in 1342. During his reign he took up the long standing conflict between the Emperor Louis of Bavaria and the Papacy, and Louis finally submitted to the Pope. Clement was more a temporal prince than an ecclesaisitcal ruler; a patron of the arts, banquets and receptions to which ladies were freely admitted. The heavy expenses necessitated by such pomp soon exhausted the funds and Clement imposed an ever-increasing number of taxes, and appointments to Bishoprics were exclusively reserved for the Pope. He died after a short illness in December 1352 in Avignon.

Pierre Roger was Bishop of Arras, Episcopus Atrabensis, and his armorial bearings show six roses.

DE MONTIBUS PAMMACHII
From the mountains of Pammachius

INNOCENT VI
1352 - 1362

STEFANO AUBERT

Stefano Aubert was born in France, and began his career as Professor of Civil Law. His career in the Church was equally spectacular; in 1342 he became Cardinal Bishop. He was elected Pope at Avignon on the 18th December 1352, where he died on the 12th September 1362.

Malachy's prophecy refers to the fact that Innocent VI had been Cardinal Priest of Pammachius. Panvinio refers to his family crest showing six hills.

GALLUS VICECOMES
A French Viscount

URBAN V
1362 - 1370

GUGLIELMO DE GRIMOARD

Guglielmo was born of a noble French family in 1310. He became a Benedictine monk and one of the greatest canonists of his day. In 1352 he became Abbot and started on a dipomatic career. Owing to jealousy within the Sacred College, which made the election of any one of its members impossible, Guglielmo De Grimoard was consecrated on the 6th November 1362 to succeed Innocent VI. He continued to wear the habit of the Benedictines. Urban was a patriotic Frenchman, which must be judged as a defect in the Pope of all Christendom; he estranged the English, aroused hostility in Italy and made many enemies. He died in Avignon on the 19th December 1370.

Malachy refers to the Pope's origin.

NOVUS DE VIRGINE FORTI
A new man from a strong virgin
[Motto also given as "Nova de virgine fortis]

GREGORY XI

1370 - 1378

PIERRE ROGER DE BEAUFORT

De Beaufort, born in 1331, was a nephew of Pope Clement VI who also created him Cardinal in 1348 when he was only eighteen years old. After the death of Urban V the Cardinals unanimously elected him Pope in Avignon in 1370. He died in 1378 in Rome.

Pierre Roger De Beaufort was Cardinal of the title of Santa Maria Nova and his name may be referred to in the word **Forti**. Another interpretation explains the legend as "renovated in spirit through the bold exhortation of the virgin Catherine of Siena".

DE INFERNO PREGNANI
(a)　The Pregnani from hell
(b)　From the hell of Pregnani

URBAN VI

1378 - 1389

BARTOLOMEO PRIGNANO

Bartolomeo was born in Naples in 1318. In 1364 he was consecrated Archbishop and after the death of Gregory XI the Conclave proposed him as candidate for the tiara. He became the first Roman Pope during the Western Schism in 1378. Urban VI is said to have died of poisoning in Rome on the 15th October 1389.

Malachy's legend is easily explained here: Urban VI was a Pregnani and a native of a place called Inferno near Naples.

CUBUS DE MIXTIONE
The square of mixture

BONIFACE IX
1389 - 1404

PIETRO TOMACELLI

Pietro who came from an ancient but impoverished noble family of Naples became the successor to the Roman Pope Urban VI on the 2nd November. The Avignon Pope, Clement VII, at the same time crowned the French Prince Louis of Anagni as King of Naples. He died in Rome on the 1st October 1404.

Malachy's prophecy is an allusion to the Pope's coat of arms, which had a bend chegny.

DE MELIORE SIDERE
From a better star

INNOCENT VII
1404 - 1406

COSMA MIGLIORATI

Born in 1336 Cosma became a Papal Delegate to England and in 1387 Archbishop of Ravenna. In 1389 Boniface IX created him Cardinal and on the 17th October 1404 he was elected Pope and took the name of Innocent VII. He died on the 6th November 1406. During his reign he did little for the suppression of the Schism.

Malachy's legend is both a play on words referring to the Pope's name and an allusion to his armorial bearings which show a comet.

NAUTA DE PONTE NIGRO
(a)   A sailor from a black bridge
(b)   The mariner of Negropont

GREGORY XII
1406 - 1415

Angelo Correr

Angelo Correr was born in 1327 in Venice. He became Bishop of Castello and Patriarch of Constantine in 1390. In 1405 he was made Cardinal and after the death of Innocent VII was elected Pope by the Cardinals in Rome on the 30th November 1406. Due to internal strifes Gregory XII resigned in 1415. The Cardinals accepted the resignation and appointed him Bishop of Porto. Two years later, before the election of a new Pope, Martin V, Gregory XII died.

Nauta appears to refer to Venice. Gregory XII was also Commendatarius of the Church of Nigripontis.

DE CRUCE APOSTOLICA
From the Apostolic Cross

CLEMENT VII (antipope)
1378 - 1394

Roberto dei Conti del Genevois

Cardinal of the title of the twelve apostles, this Pope's coat of arms shows a cross, quarterly pierced. He is responsible for the Great Schism of the West, a period in the history of the Church which lasted for nearly half a century.

LUNA COSMEDINA
The Moon of Cosmedin

BENEDICT XIII (ANTIPOPE)
1394 - 1423

PETER DE LUNA

This pope was the famous Peter De Luna, Cardinal of the title of St Mary in Cosmedina, who was born in 1328 and created Cardinal in 1375. He returned to Rome with Gregory XI after whose death he took part in the conclave which was attacked by the Romans and which elected Urban VI. His spiritual director and confessor was the great Vincent Ferrer, who believed him to be the real Pope. When Clement VII died he was unanimously chosen to succeed him. He died in Spain in 1423.

Malachy's description refers both to the antipope's name and his coat of arms.

SCHISMA BARCHINONICUM
The Schism of Barcelona

CLEMENT VIII (ANTIPOPE)
1423 - 1429

GIL SANCHEZ MUNOZ

This Pope is only recorded in a footnote to the Vatican list. However, Panvinio ranks him among the real Popes but adds "Sedit seu instrusus fuit". He was a Canon of Barcelona to which Malachy's description alludes and died in 1447.

[In the same footnote appears the name Bernardo Garnier who claimed the title Benedict XIV between 1425 and 1430.]

FLAGELLUM SOLIS
The lash of the sun

ALEXANDER V (ANTIPOPE)
1409 - 1410

PIETRO FILARGO

Piero, born in 1339, was a homeless begger boy in a Cretan city, knowing neither parents nor relations. He received elementary education from a friar and later entered a Franciscan monastery. Because of his unusual ability he was sent to be educated at Oxford and Paris where he distinguished himself as professor, preacher and writer. Pietro was made Bishop in 1386 and Pope Innocent VII made him a Cardinal in 1405. On the 26th June 1409 he was the unanimous choice of the Cardinals to fill the presumably vacant papal chair. His pontificate was marked by unsuccessful efforts to reach Rome. He died on 3rd May 1410 in Bologna, where he was held prisoner by Cardinal Cossa who succeeded Alexander V as John XXIII, on the 3rd May 1410.

CERVUS SIRENÆ
The Stag of the Syren

JOHN XXIII (ANTIPOPE)
1410 - 1415

BALDASSARRE COSSA

Baldassarre was born in 1370 and was one of the seven Cardinals who, in 1408, deserted Gregory XII and who had pleced themselves under the jurisdiction of Benedict XIII. He became Cardinal in 1402 and Papal Legate in the following year. In 1409 Cossa played an important part in the Council of Pisa and when Popes Gregory XII and Benedict XIII were deposed, he conducted the election of Alexander V who remained entirely under his influence. He died on the 22nd November 1419.

Malachy's prophecy is an allusion to the fact that Cossa became Cardinal of the title of St Eustachius, who has the stag as an emblem. He was born in Naples which has the emblem of the syren.

COLUMNA VELI AUREI
The pillar with the golden veil

MARTIN V

1417 - 1431

ODDONE COLONNA

Oddone Colonna was born in 1368 and became a Papal Nuncio at various Italian courts under Boniface IX. In 1405 he was made a Cardinal (Velabro). He deserted Pope Gregory XII and participated in the election of the Antipopes Alexander V and John XXIII. The influential family of Colonna had already given twenty-seven Cardinals to the Church, but Martin V was the first to ascend to the Papal throne. The Church was just passing through the most critical period of its history, the great Western Schism. John XXIII had submitted to Pope Martin in 1419 and was given the title of Cardinal Bishop of Frascati. He died in Rome in 1431.

Malachy's prophecy is an allusion to the pope's cardinal title and his family name.

LUPA CŒLESTINA
The Cœlestinian she-wolf

E U G E N E I V
1431 - 1447

GABRIELE CONDULMER

Gabriele was born at Venice in 1383 and was the nephew of Gregory XII. Although he inherited a vast fortune, he gave it away to the poor and entered a monastery. At the age of twenty-four he was appointed by his uncle as Bishop of Siena. In 1408 he was created Cardinal and became Pope in 1431. He died in Rome in 1447.

Malachy refers in his legend to the fact that Eugene IV belonged to the order of the Celestines and also was Bishop of Siena which bears a she-wolf on its arms.

AMATOR CRUCIS
A lover of the Cross

F E L I X V (ANTIPOPE)
1439 - 1449

AMADEUS DUKE OF SAVOY

Amadeus was born in 1383. After the schismatic Council of Basle had declared the rightful pope, Eugene IV, deposed, the Cardinals wished to secure additional influence and financial support by turning to the rich and powerful Prince, the Duke Amadeus VIII of Savoy. After the death of his wife Maria of Burgundy, Duke Amadeus led a life of contemplation, in the company of five knights whom he had formed into the Order of St Maurice. He was consecrated and crowned by Cardinal d'Allamand in 1440. He submitted in 1449 to Nicholas V from whom he received the title of Cardinal of St Sabina. He died in 1451.

FELICE V	**NICCOLÒ V**	**CALLISTO III**	**PIO II**
1439 *antip.* 1449	1447 1455	1455 1458	1458 1464
AMEDEO DUCA DI SAVOIA	TOMMASO PARENTUCELLI	ALFONSO BORGIA	ENEA SILVIO PICCOLOMINI
PAOLO II	**SISTO IV**	**INNOCENZO VIII**	**ALESSANDRO VI**
1464 1471	1471 1484	1484 1492	1492 1503
PIETRO BARBO	FRANCESCO DELLA ROVERE	GIOVANNI BATTISTA CIBO	RODRIGO BORGIA
PIO III	**GIULIO II**	**LEONE X**	**ADRIANO VI**
1503 1503	1503 1513	1513 1521	1522 1523
FRANCESCO TODE-SCHINI-PICCOLOMINI	GIULIANO DELLA ROVERE	GIOVANNI DE' MEDICI	ADRIANO FLORENSZ
CLEMENTE VII	**PAOLO III**	**GIULIO III**	**MARCELLO II**
1523 1534	1534 1549	1550 1555	1555 1555
GIULIO DE' MEDICI	ALESSANDRO FARNESE	GIOVANNI MARIA CIOCCHI DEL MONTE	MARCELLO CERVINI
PAOLO IV	**PIO IV**	**S. PIO V**	**GREGORIO XIII**
1555 1559	1559 1565	1566 1572	1572 1585
GIAN PIETRO CARAFA	GIOVAN ANGELO DE' MEDICI	ANTONIO (MICHELE) GHISLIERI	UGO BONCOMPAGNI

DE MODICITATE LUNÆ
From the littleness of the moon

NICHOLAS V
1447 - 1455

TOMMASO PARENTUCELLI

Tommaso was born in 1397 and acted as the factotum of the Bishop of Bologna for twenty years. He accompanied the Bishop on many missions and later became the protegé of Eugene IV who also entrusted him with other diplomatic tasks, which he carried out with such success that he received the Cardinal's hat in 1446. After the death of Pope Eugene, Parentucelli was elected Pope. He died in Rome in 1455.

Malachy's prophecy refers to his place of birth in the diocese of Luna and his humble origin.

BOS PASCENS
(a)   an ox feeding
(b)   a bull browsing

CALIXTUS III
1455 - 1458

ALFONSO BORGIA

Alfonso was born in 1378 of a noble family and after finishing his studies espoused the cause of Benedict XIII who created him a Canon. He submitted, however, to Martin V who appointed him Bishop of Valencia in 1429 and Eugene IV made him a Cardinal in 1444. In 1455 Alfonso de Borgia was elected Pope. His reign is remarkable for the revision of the trial of Joan of Arc, which was carried out by his directions and according to which the sentence of the first court was quashed and her innocence proclaimed. He was probably one of the richest Popes in history and died at Rome in 1458.

Malachy's prophecy is an allusion to the Pope's armorial bearing which shows the ox of the Borgias.

DE CAPRA ET ALBERGO
(Another version reads CUPRA)

P I U S I I
1458 - 1464

ENEA SILVIO PICCOLOMINI

This pope was also born of a noble family, in 1405. He received elementary instruction from a priest and entered the University of Siena at the age of eighteen. He became the secretary to Bishop Capranica and later to the antipope Felix V. In 1445 he changed his allegiance and in 1447 became Bishop of Trieste. In 1456 he was created a Cardinal by Calixtus III whom he succeeded as Pope in 1458. He died on the 14th August 1464.

Malachy's description has been interpreted as being an allusion to the fact that Pius II had been secretary to Cardinal Capranica and Cardinal Albergato before he was elected Pope.

DE CERVO ET LEONE
From a stag and a lion

P A U L I I
1464 - 1471

PIETRO BARBO

Pietro Barbo, a nephew of Eugene IV, was born in Venice in 1417 and entered the religious profession at the elevation of his uncle to the papacy. He was first Bishop of Cervia and Cardinal of Venice. He succeeded Pius II as Pope in 1464 and died in 1471.

Malachy refers to his Bishopric Cervia (stag) and his Cardinal title of St Mark (lion).

PISCATOR MINORITA
The Minorite Fisherman

S I X T U S   I V
1471 - 1484

Francesco della Rovere

Francesco was born in 1414. As a child he was placed in a Franciscan monastery because of the poverty of his parents. After filling the post of Procurator of his order in Rome, he was in 1467 created Cardinal by Paul II. He was elected Pope in 1471. His reign was overshadowed by political strifes and quarrels in which members of his family played leading parts and his appointing of men such as Pietro and Girolamo Riario to the highest offices in the Church are blots on his high office. He died in 1484.

Francesco was born the son of a fisherman and a member of the Minor Friars. [It is interesting to note that at the time of Malachy this Order did not exist.]

PRÆCURSOR SICILIÆ
(a)   The Precursor of Sicily
(b)   The forerunner from Sicily

I N N O C E N T   V I I I
1484 - 1492

Giovanni Battista Cibo

Giovanni was born in 1432 and entered the service of the Church after a somewhat licentious youth. In 1467 he became Bishop and in 1484 the successor to Sixtus IV. Great insecurity reigned at Rome during his rule, largely owing to weakness on his part in dealing with transgressors. In 1484 he issued his much abused Bull against witchcraft. Constantly confronted with financial difficulties he resorted to the objectionable habit of creating new offices and granting them to the highest bidders. A great number of Papal Bulls were sold during his reign, many of which are considered to be forgeries: among these latter must be placed the permission granted to the Norwegians to celebrate Mass without wine.

The only explanation Malachy's interpretors can give is that he spent much time at the court of the King of Sicily. Other explanations appear somewhat far-fetched, such as that the forerunner (Precursor) of Jesus was called John the Baptist which happened to be also the Pope's name.

BOS ALBANUS IN PORTU
The Alban bull at the port

A L E X A N D E R   V I
1492 - 1503

RODRIGO BORGIA

The young Rodrigo who was born in Spain on the 1st January 1431, had not yet chosen his profession when the elevation of his uncle to the Papacy (1455) opened up new prospects to his ambition. His uncle conferred upon him rich benefices and sent him to study law at the University of Bologna. In 1456 he was made a Cardinal and he held the titles of Cardinal Bishop of Albano and Porto. Towards 1470 began his relations with Venozza Catanei, the mother of his four children: Juan, Caesar, Lucrezia and Jofre.

Borgia, by a two-thirds majority which was secured by his own vote, became Pope in 1492, and took the name of Alexander VI. He is probably the only Pope who has never found an apologist in spite of the most grievous accusations against him by his contemporaries. Perhaps the kindest thing one can do is to use the words of Leo the Great (440-461) who had declared in his *Third Homily for Christmas Day* that "The dignity of Peter suffers no diminution even in an unworthy successor". Alexander VI died in Rome on the 18th August 1503.

Malachy's prophecy refers to the pope's armorial bearings and his Cardinal titles of Albano and Porto.

DE PARVO HOMINE
From a little man

PIUS III
1503

FRANCESCO TODESCHINI-PICCOLOMINI

Francesco who was a nephew of Pope Pius II, was born in 1439. He had spent his boyhood in destitute circumstances when his uncle took him into his household, bestowed upon him his family name and arms and took charge of his training and education. His uncle appointed him Archbishop of Siena and in 1460 created him Cardinal. After the death of Alexander VI the Cardinals could not agree on a principal candidate and cast their vote in favour of Piccolomini, who though only 64 years old died after a reign of only 26 days, in 1503.

Malachy refers to his family name Piccolomini (parvus homo), in English: little man.

FRUCTUS JOVIS JUVABIT
The fruit of Jupiter will help

JULIUS II
1503 - 1513

GIULIANO DELLA ROVERE

Giuliano della Rovere was born in 1443. He followed his uncle into the Franciscan Order and, after his uncle's elevation to the Papacy as Sixtus IV in 1471, began his public career. In 1471 he was created a Cardinal and held numerous episcopal sees. After the death of Sixtus IV in 1484 Cardinal Rovere played a disreputable role in the election of Innocent VIII. Seeing that his own chances for the Papacy were unfavourable he secured the election of a Pope likely to be a puppet in his hands. After the death of Alexander VI he was again a strong candidate, but he had to allow the sick Piccolomini to become Pope before he was able to secure the Cardinals' votes for himself by bribery and promises. (It was the shortest conclave in the history of the Papacy). Julius II spent money liberally on the erection of magnificent palaces and fortresses. Before he became Pope he was the father of three daughters, one of whom, Felice, he gave in marriage to Giovanni Orsini in 1506. He died in 1513.

The Latin legend (*Fructus Jovis Juvabit*) is a reference to the Pope's armorial bearings. On his arms was an oak tree which was the sacred tree to Jupiter.

DE CRATICULA POLITIANA
From a Politian "gridiron"

LEO X
1513 - 1521

GIOVANNI DE' MEDICI

Giovanni de' Medici was born in 1475 son of Lorenzo de' Medici (the Magnificent) and appointed a Cardinal at the age of thirteen. His educator and mentor was the most distinguished humanist and scholar, Angelo Politiano. In 1494 he had to flee his native city in the habit of a Franciscan monk and made several fruitless attempts to restore the supremacy of his family in Florence. The Medicis returned to favour in 1512 and in 1513 Giovanni, then thirty-seven years old, was elected Pope. During his reign he spent nearly five million ducats and left his successor with a debt of nearly half a million ducats. His creditors faced financial ruin and contemporary publications proclaim "Leo X has consumed three pontificates, the treasure of Julius

61

II, the revenues of his own reign and those of his successor". He died at Rome in 1521.

"*Craticula*", the "gridiron" refers to his father Laurence the Magnificent and *Politiana* to his mentor. This is by any standard a strange way of describing a person.

LEO FLORENTI(N)US
The lion of Florence

A D R I A N   V I
1522 - 1523

ADRIANO FLORENSZ

He is the only Pope of modern times, except Marcellus II, who retained his baptismal name. Born of humble parentage in Utrecht in 1459, his education was sponsored by his mother and also Margaret of Burgundy. In 1506 he became the tutor to the grandson of Emperor Maximillian, the future Charles V. Within the next decade he became Bishop, Grand Inquisitor, Cardinal and finally Regent of Spain. In 1522 the Cardinals elected him unanimously to succeed Pope Leo X. Adrian VI died on the 14th September 1523.

Malachy's legend refers to his family name and to the fact that two lions adorn his arms.

FLOS PILEI ÆGRI
The flower of the ball

C L E M E N T   V I I
1523 - 1534

GIULIO DE' MEDICI

Born in 1478 a few days after the death of his father, Giulio was educated by his uncle Laurence the Magnificent. After his cousin's elevation to the Papacy as Leo X, many honours were bestowed upon him and in 1513 he was made a Cardinal. After Adrian's death Cardinal de' Medici was eventually chosen Pope. He was an Italian Prince, a diplomat first and a spiritual ruler afterwards. He died in 1534.

Flos Pilei Ægri is a reference to the Pope's armorial bearings; on his arms were six torteaux, the top one of which was charged with three fleurs-de-lis. It is during this Pope's reign that the divorce of Katherine of Aragon and Henry VIII's revolt against the Church took place.

HYACINTHUS MEDICORUM
The hyacinth of physicians

PAUL III
1534 - 1549

ALESSANDRO FARNESE

Alessandro was born at Rome in 1468 of an ancient Roman family with a long tradition of service to the Church. His grandfather was commander-in-chief of Papal troops under Eugene IV. Alessandro had an excellent education and with such advantages as birth and talent his advancement in the Church was assured and rapid. In 1493 Alexander VI created him a Cardinal with the title of St Cosmas and Damian. He was a Cardinal for over forty years and finally became Dean of the Sacred College. In 1534 the conclave proclaimed him successor to Clement VII without the formality of a ballot. During his reign a number of religious orders were founded, of which the Jesuits and Ursulines are the best known. He died in 1549.

Earlier interpreters give the Pope's arms as charged with six hyacinths. He was also Cardinal of the title of St Cosmas and Damian, who were both doctors. Malachy's legend appears to refer to these two facts.

DE CORONA MONTANA
Of the mountain crown

J U L I U S   I I I
1550 - 1555

Giammaria M. Ciocchi del Monte

Giammaria was born on the 10th September 1487 and studied under the Dominicans. In 1512 he succeeded his uncle Antonio del Monte as Archbishop of Siponto. Under Clement VII he was twice appointed Prefect of Rome and after the sack of the City (1527) was one of the hostages given by Clement VII to the Imperialists. Paul III created him a Cardinal in 1536 and he became the successor to that Pope in 1550 after a conclave of ten weeks. His inactivity during the last three years of his pontificate was caused by frequent and severe attacks of gout. The great blemish in his reign was Nepotism: shortly after his accession he created a youth of seventeen, whom he had picked up in the streets of Palma, a Cardinal. He was also extremely lavish in bestowing ecclesiastical honours and benefices upon his relatives. On the 23rd March 1555 he died in Rome.

Malachy's legend refers to the Pope's armorial bearings: his arms showed laurel crowns and mountains.

FRUMENTUM FLOCCIDUM
(a)   Hairy grain
(b)   Useless corn

M A R C E L L U S   I I
1555

Marcello Cervini

Marcello was born in 1501 and had a spectacular career as Papal secretary, which position offered him great influence in the papal

Curia. Pope Paul III created him a Cardinal in 1539. In 1545 he was appointed one of the three Presidents of the Council of Trent and in 1548 he became Librarian of the Vatican. He was also Bishop of Nicastro and Reggio. After the death of Julius III the thirty-nine Cardinals of the conclave elected Cardinal Cervini to the papacy; however, he died after a reign of only twenty-two days.

Palestrina entitled one of his famous polyphonic masses *Missa Papæ Marcelli* in his honour. The Pope's arms show ears of wheat, while the other reference obviously alludes to the shortness of his pontificate.

DE FIDE PETRI
Of the faith of Peter

P A U L I V
1555 - 1559

GIOVANNI PIETRO CARAFFA

The family into which Giovanni was born in 1476 was one of the most illustrious in Naples and he was introduced to the Papal court in 1494 by his famous uncle Cardinal Oliviero Caraffa. Leo X appointed him Ambassador to England and also retained him as Nuncio in Spain. In 1536 he became Cardinal and later Archbishop of Naples. In 1555 he was elected Pope and Nepotism once again reigned supreme.

EDITOR'S NOTE

Onoviro Panvinio, the historian, died at Palermo on the 7th April, 1568. Pope Paul IV is the last Pope mentioned in his epitome. With his death, the prophecies of St Malachy lose an interpreter of great stature. In his lifetime Panvinio had collected with meticulous thoroughness many details and historical facts about the Popes' lives; he often supplied armorial bearings of the Popes' family and facts which were of the greatest help to other interpreters of Malachy.

During his unfortunate reign occurred the final break between the Church of Rome and England. His pontificate was a great disappointment: he who at the beginning was honoured by a public statue lived to see it thrown down and mutilated by the hostile population of Rome. On the 18th August 1559 he died, and was buried in St Peters, but his body was later transferred to another church.

Paul IV appears to have been better known by his Christian name Pietro; Caraffa is derived from the Latin *cara fides*.

ÆSCULAPII PHARMACUM
(a)   The medicine of Æsculapius
(b)   The Æsculapius of doctors

PIUS IV
1559 - 1565

GIOVANNI ANGELO DE' MEDICI

This pope was born at Milan in 1499. The Medicis of Milan lived in very humble circumstances and the proud house of Florence of the same name claimed no kindred with them until Cardinal Medici was seated on the Papal throne. After his studies in his twenty eighth year he went to Rome where his talents were appreciated by successive Popes. In the last year of Paul III's reign he was created a Cardinal and Julius III appointed him Commander of the Papal troops. His hostility towards Paul IV worked out to his advantage because the conclave which had assembled to elect that Pope's successor voted for the man who in every respect was Paul's opposite. By acclamation he was pronounced Pope in 1560. He died in 1565.

Malachy's legend appears to be a reference to the Pope's family name, but most interpreters point out that the young Medici had studied medicine and was a qualified doctor.

ANGELUS NEMOROSUS
(a)   The angel of the wood
(b)   The angel of Bosco

PIUS V

1566 - 1572

ANTONIO MICHELE GHISLERI

Born of a poor family in 1504 Antonio was educated by the Dominicans and entered that religious order in 1528. Pope Paul IV made him a Bishop in 1556 and a Cardinal in 1557. In the same year he was appointed Inquisitor General for all Christendom. When Pius IV wished to admit a thirteen year old boy into the Sacred College, Cardinal Ghisleri opposed and defeated the Pope and his plans. In 1566 he was elected Pontiff. He died in 1572. During his reign he excommunicated Queen Elizabeth I of England and wrote a letter to Mary Stuart in prison.

The Latin legend refers to the Pope's Christian name Michele (Angelus) and his birthplace (Bosco) Lombardy. *

It is important to realise that a number of interpreters of the prophecies were Italians, for some prophecies contain a play upon Italian words. They are unfortunately never explained.

---

* It is important to note that Italian interpreters never give an explanation when the prophecies contain a play upon Italian words. This occurs quite frequently.

. . . .

GREGORY XIII
1572 - 1585

Ugo Boncompagni

Ugo was born at Bologna in 1502. He studied law and was appointed Judge of the Capitol by Pope Paul III. Paul IV appointed him a Bishop and Pius IV created him a Cardinal in 1564. After the death of Pius V in 1572 he was elected Pope. His main efforts were concentrated on restoring the Catholic faith in those countries that had become Protestant. Historians have severly criticised Gregory XIII for the massacre of the Huguenots on St Bartholomew's day in 1572. No other act of Gregory XIII has gained for him a more lasting fame than his reform of the Julian calendar which was introduced in 1578. He died at Rome in 1585.

Malachy's interpreters give as an explanation for *Medium Corpus Pilarum* the fact that on his shield was a dragon naissant, and that Gregory XIII was created a Cardinal by Pius V who had six Torteaux (Pilias) on his Coat of Arms.

AXIS IN MEDIETATE SIGNI
An axis in the midst of the sign

SIXTUS V
1585 - 1590

Felice Peretti

Felice was born the son of a gardener in 1521 and it is said of him that as a boy he worked as a swineherd. When nine years old he joined a convent where he was educated and ordained Priest in 1547. He soon became famous as a preacher and Pope Pius IV appointed him Counsellor to the Inquisition at Venice. In 1566 he was created a Bishop by Pius V and in 1570 Cardinal. In 1585 he was elected

SISTO V	**URBANO VII**	**GREGORIO XIV**	**INNOCENZO IX**
1585 — 1590	1590 — 1590	1590 — 1591	1591 — 1591
FELICE PERETTI	GIOVANNI BATTISTA CASTAGNA	NICCOLÒ SFONDRATI	GIOVANNI ANTONIO FACCHINETTI
CLEMENTE VIII	**LEONE XI**	**PAOLO V**	**GREGORIO XV**
1592 — 1605	1605 — 1605	1605 — 1621	1621 — 1623
IPPOLITO ALDOBRANDINI	ALESSANDRO DE' MEDICI	CAMILLO BORGHESE	ALESSANDRO LUDOVISI
URBANO VIII	**INNOCENZO X**	**ALESSANDRO VII**	**CLEMENTE IX**
1623 — 1644	1644 — 1655	1655 — 1667	1667 — 1669
MAFFEO BARBERINI	GIOVANNI BATTISTA PAMPHILJ	FABIO CHIGI	GIULIO ROSPIGLIOSI
CLEMENTE X	**B. INNOCENZO XI**	**ALESSANDRO VIII**	**INNOCENZO XII**
1670 — 1676	1676 — 1689	1689 — 1691	1691 — 1700
EMILIO ALTIERI	BENEDETTO ODESCALCHI	PIETRO OTTOBONI	ANTONIO PIGNATELLI
CLEMENTE XI	**INNOCENZO XIII**	**BENEDETTO XIII**	**CLEMENTE XII**
1700 — 1721	1721 — 1724	1724 — 1730	1730 — 1740
GIAN FRANCESCO ALBANI	MICHELANGELO DEI CONTI	PIETRO FRANCESCO ORSINI	LORENZO CORSINI

Pope after a conclave of four days. After a reign of five years he died in 1590.

Malachy's prophecy is a straightforward allusion to the Pope's coat of arms.

DE RORE CŒLI
From the dew of heaven

URBAN VII
1590

Giovanni Battista Castagna

Giovanni Battista was born at Rome in 1521 and was a nephew of Cardinal Jacovazzi. He studied civl and canon law and graduated as a doctor of both. In 1553 he was appointed Archbishop of Rossano and Julius III sent him as Governor to Fano in 1555. In 1573 he resigned his See and Gregory XIII sent him as Nuncio to Venice. In 1583 he was made a Cardinal. Three years later he became Inquisitor General of the Holy Office. He was elected Pope in 1590, on the 15th September, and his reign lasted only 13 days. He died on the 27th September 1590.

Urban VII had been Bishop of Rossano in Calabria where manna called "the dew of heaven" is gathered. (Manna is a sweetish secretion from many trees — as the Manna Ash etc.).

EX ANTIQUITATE URBIS
From the old city

GREGORY XIV
1590 - 1591

Niccolo' Sfondrati

Niccolò was born near Milan in 1553. His father Francisco, a Milanese senator, was, after the death of his wife, created a Cardinal by Pope Paul III in 1544. Niccolò was ordained priest and then appointed Bishop of Cremona in 1560. Gregory XIII created him Cardinal Priest of Santa Cecilia in 1583. In 1590 he succeeded Urban VII as Pope. He died in 1591.

De Antiquitate Urbis is another reading of Malachy's legend. It has been suggested that this particular reference in the prophecies was forged during the Conclave by partisans of Cardinal Simon Celli, and was turned into Bishop of Orvieto, in Latin "Urbevetanum — old city"; thus the prophecy was supposed to point out by the above legend that it was the will of providence that this Cardinal be elected Pope. The attempt failed because another Cardinal was elected: Niccolò, from the city of Milan. The explanation was then given that Gregory XIV was a son and grandson of Senators of the city of Milan. Senator comes from the Latin "senex", old man. *De Antiquitate Urbis* could mean "from the ancient of the city". However it could also be said that Milan is an old city having been founded in 400 B.C.

PIA CIVITAS IN BELLO
The pious city at war

INNOCENT IX
1591

GIOVANNI ANTONIO FACCHINETTI

Born in 1519 Giovanni became secretary to a Roman Cardinal and in 1560 Bishop. In 1575 he was appointed Patriarch of Jerusalem and in 1583 created Cardinal of the title of the Four Crowned Martyrs. During the reign of Gregory XIV much of the burden of the Papal administration rested on his shoulders and on the Pontiff's death he was raised to the Papacy. He died in 1591.

Malachy's legend obviously refers to the city of Jerusalem of which the Cardinal was Patriarch before succeeding to the Papacy.

CRUX ROMULEA
The Roman cross

CLEMENT VIII
1592 - 1605

IPPOLITO ALDOBRANDINI

Ippolito was born in 1536. His career was spectacular and he became Cardinal in 1585. His spiritual mentor had been Phillip Neri who remained his confessor for over thirty years. On his elevation to the Papacy Baronius became the Pope's confessor. He died in 1605. The adjective Romulus, meaning Roman, is also mentioned in one of the hymns of the Breviary. The Pope's coat of arms show an embattled bend which is also referred to as a Roman cross. Abbé Cucherat refers to the "cross of Ireland" Clement VIII had to bear at this time because she remained faithful to Rome. There has always been a very special regard for this Pope by the Irish. [During this Pope's reign the twenty-six martyrs of Japan were crucified; their canonisation was reserved for the Pope to whom Malachy had given the description *Crux de Cruce.*]

UNDOSUS VIR
(a)   A billowy man
(b)   Disappearing like the waves of the sea

LEO XI
1605

ALESSANDRO OTTAVIANO DE' MEDICI

De' Medici was born at Florence in 1535. He became ambassador to Pius V, representing the Duke of Tuscany, which position he held for fifteen years. Gregory XIII made him a Bishop in 1573, Archbishop of Florence in 1574 and Cardinal in 1583. After the death of Clement VIII he was elected Pope, but he died twenty-seven days after his election in 1605.

It has been suggested that Malachy referred to the Pope's short reign. Although not borne out by his Papal coat of arms *"Undosus Vir"* is likely to be an allusion to his heraldic design. A Dutch interpreter of the prophecies of Malachy translates the motto as "A Waterman". There is no explanation concerning Malachy's legend which is completely satisfactory.

GENS PERVERSA
The wicked race

P A U L   V
1605 - 1621

CAMILLO BORGHESE

Born in 1550 Camillo's career in the Church was not spectacular. In 1596 he was made a Cardinal by Clement VIII and was appointed Cardinal Vicar of Rome. He was elected Pope in 1605. In 1606 Paul V wrote a letter to James I of England, congratulating him on his succession to the throne, expressing his grief about the plot recently made against the monarch's life and begging the King of England not to make the innocent Catholics suffer for the crime of a few. He promised to exhort all the governors of the realm to be submissive and loyal to their sovereign in all things not opposed to the honour of God. Unfortunately the oath of allegiance demanded by James of his subjects contained clauses which had to be solemnly condemned by the Pope in 1607. This condemnation occasioned the bitter dissension between the monarchy and those governors who submitted to the decision of the Pope. Pope Paul V died in 1621.

The most obvious explanation of Malachy's legend is an allusion to the Pope's armorial bearings which show a dragon and an eagle. These were often referred to as the *Gens Perversa*. There is another interpretation which refers to the war between the Ghibelines and Guelphs whose crests were the dragon and the eagle.

IN TRIBULATIONE PACIS
In the disturbance of peace

GREGORY XV
1621 - 1623

ALESSANDRO LUDOVISI

Alessandro was born in 1554, and became a Judge of the Capitol. In 1612 Paul V appointed him Archbishop of Bologna and it was he who, as Nuncio to Savoy, had to mediate between the Duke of Savoy and King Philip of Spain. In 1616 he was created Cardinal and he was elected successor to Pope Paul V in 1621. The relations between England and the Roman See assumed a more friendly character during his pontificate and Gregory XV was respected by the rulers of the continent, not only in religious affairs but also in matters of a purely political nature. He died in 1623.

Malachy's prophecy is an obvious reference to the Pope's activities as Nuncio which were mainly concerned with the restoration of disturbances which might well have lead to wars.

It is true to say that all the prophecies since Urban VII (1590) are somewhat vague; this has lead critics of the prophecies to suggest that they were indeed forgeries of Cardinal Simon Celli.

LILIUM ET ROSA
The lily and the rose

URBAN VIII
1623 - 1644

MATTEO BARBERINI

He was born in 1568 and educated under the Jesuits. In 1601 he was appointed Papal Legate to France and in 1604 Archbishop of Nazareth. Later he was sent as Nuncio to Paris and in 1606 he was made a Cardinal by Paul V. He was elected Pope in 1623 and throughout his reign he concerned himself with the affairs of France and England. He died in 1644.

There have been many interpretations of Malachy's legend which appear to be a reference to armorial bearings. There is no doubt that his particular interest in the affairs of France (fleur de lis) and England (the rose) seems the most obvious explanation.

JUCUNDITAS CRUCIS
The joy of the cross

INNOCENT X
1644 - 1655

GIOVANNI BATTISTA PAMPHILJ

Born in 1574 he became Nuncio at Naples and a Cardinal in 1626. He was elected Pope in 1644. He died in 1655. It is interesting to note that Innocent X was raised to the Pontificate after a long and difficult Conclave on the Feast of the Exaltation of the Cross.

MONTIUM CUSTOS
The guardian of the hills

ALEXANDER VII
1655 - 1667

FABIO CHIGI

Fabio was born in 1599 of one of the most illustrious and powerful Italian families. He entered upon his ecclesiastical career in 1626 and held many posts and responsibilities. In 1651 he became Secretary of State to Innocent X who made him a Cardinal in 1652. In the Conclave of 1655, which lasted eighty days and which is famous for the clash of nation and faction, Chigi was unanimously elected Pope. He died in 1667.

Malachy's legend is an obvious allusion to the Pope's armorial bearings.

SYDUS OLORUM
(a)   A star of the swans
(b)   The constellation of swans

CLEMENT IX
1667 - 1669

GIULIO ROSPIGLIOSI

Born in 1600 Giulio enjoyed the special favour of Urban VIII who made him Archibishop of Tarsus and sent him as Nuncio to the Spanish Court. In 1657 Alexander VII appointed him Cardinal and ten years later he was elected to the See of St Peter. In 1668 he declared Rose of Lima to be the first American Saint. He died at Rome in December 1669.

The Pope's family came originally from Lombardy where its ancient history is well recorded. The *Teatro Araldico*, a work which gives the armorial bearings of the most ancient and noble families of Italy, describes the Pope's family coat of arms as a shield on which was emblazoned a swan with stars overhead. Another seventeenth century interpretation is that during the conclave this Pope occupied a room which was known as the Chamber of Swans.

DE FLUMINE MAGNO
From the great river

CLEMENT X
1670 - 1676

EMILIO ALTIERI

Emilio was born in 1590, and had a quite unspectacular career in the Church. Clement IX created him Cardinal when he was in his eighties. Unable to secure the election of any of the prominent candidates the Cardinals, after a Conclave of nearly five months, decided on electing a Cardinal of advanced years. Thus Clement X became pontiff. He died in 1676.

Malachy's prophecy concerning this Pope has two possible interpretations: Clement X was born at Rome and in July 1590 the unusual phenomena of the Tiber overflowing its banks is given in Moréri's interpretations of the prophecies. The other explanation is that Malachy's reference is simply a play on words concerning the Pope's name which was Altieri (Alto Reo — a deep river); however, the latter appears to be rather obscure.

BELLUA INSATIABILIS
An insatiable beast

INNOCENT XI
1676 - 1689

BENEDETTO ODESCALCHI

Born in 1611. Benedetto was created a Cardinal by Innnocent X. He was a strong candidate for the Papacy after the death of Clement IX, but the French Government rejected him. After the death of Clement X, King Louis XIV of France again intended to use his real influence against Cardinal Odescalchi's election, but the King yielded to the pressure of the Conclave and after an interregnum of two months he was unanimously elected in 1676 to the Papacy. He died in 1689.

Malachy's legend may be a reference to the Pope's armorial bearings which show a lion and a bird of prey both of which had the reputation of being insatiable beasts. However, contemporary interpreters gave a different explanation of *Bellua Insatiabilis*. It is known that Innocent XI was entirely guided by the views of Cardinal Cibo and this circumstance gave rise to a pun that Innocent XI was "Insatiabilis" for he was never *sine Cibo*, "without Cibo" or "without food".

PŒNITENTIA GLORIOSA
Glorious repentance

ALEXANDER VIII
1689 - 1691

PIETRO OTTOBONI

Pietro Ottoboni was born in 1610. He enjoyed all the wealth and social position of a descendant of one of the most noble families of Venice. He was made a Cardinal in 1652 and elected to the Papacy in 1689. He died in 1691.

Cucherat thinks that the prophecy refers to the submission and consequent repentance of the Gallican Bishops.

RASTRUM IN PORTA
The rake of the door

INNOCENT XII
1691 - 1700

ANTONIO PIGNATELLI

Born in 1615 Antonio entered the Roman Curia at the age of twenty. In 1682 he was made a Cardinal and in 1687 Archbishop of Naples. As a compromise the Conclave chose Cardinal Pignatelli to succeed Alexander VIII. He died in 1700.

It is difficult to find a satisfactory explanation for this legend. *Rastrum* means "at hand" or "the next coming on". It could also mean a rake. This word has undergone many changes of meaning in the course of the last five centuries. In 1582 a dictionary description refers to "a very lean person", and a translation of 1653 gives as the meaning "somebody dissolute" or 'fond of fashion". Such speculation is by no mean satisfactory and does not supply a straightforward interpretation of Malachy's prophecy — it is simply guess work.

FLORES CIRCUMDATI
Surrounded with flowers

CLEMENT XI
1700 - 1721

GIOVANNI FRANCESCO ALBANI

Giovanni was born in 1649 and at the age of twenty-eight was made a Prelate. In 1690 he was created a Cardinal and the Conclave of 1700 chose him, after deliberating for forty-six days, to be the successor to Innocent XII. He died in 1721.

Urbino, the city where the Pope was born, has a garland of flowers on its coat of arms. It is interesting to note that during the reign of Clement XI a coin was struck and on the exergue were the words "Flores Circumdati". There is no doubt that those who had the medal struck must have been mindful of the prophecies of Malachy which had become not only common property since 1595, but were extremely popular at that time.

DE BONA RELIGIONE
From a good religious background

INNOCENT XIII
1721 - 1724

MICHELANGELO DEI CONTI

He was born in 1655, the son of Carlo II, Duke of Poli. He was created a Cardinal in 1706, and held various offices until in 1721 he was elected Pope in a stormy Conclave. He died in 1724.

This Pope belonged to the famous Conti family which has given so many Popes to the Church. Malachy's legend could therefore be translated "Of a good religious family". This explanation is shared by many medieval interpreters.

MILES IN BELLO
The soldier in battle

BENEDICT XIII
1724 - 1730

PIETRO FRANCESCO ORSINI

Born in 1649, he entered the Dominican order at the age of sixteen against the will of his parents. They appealed in vain to

Clement IX. At the age of twenty-one he was promoted to a professorship and in 1672 elevated to the position of Cardinal. In 1686 a serious illness caused his transfer to Benevento where he remained for thirty-eight years until he was elected Pope in 1724. His first concern as Pope was to enforce rigidly ecclesiastical discipline and he was unsparing in his efforts to abolish luxury and worldly pomp among the Cardinals.

Malachy's legend has always been interpreted to refer to the Pope's constant battle against the pomp and worldly interests of the Curia.

COLUMNA EXCELSA
A lofty pillar

CLEMENT XII
1730 - 1740

LORENZO CORSINI

Lorenzo was born in 1652 and the number of members of his family who had risen to high positions in the Church is innumerable. In 1691 he became Archbishop and Nuncio of Vienna. In 1756 he was created a Cardinal and made Papal Treasurer. His elevation to the Papacy in 1730 caused no surprise. In the second year of his Pontificate he became totally blind. He died in his eighty-eighth year in 1740.

Cucherat interprets the prophecy as an allusion to a bronze statue erected by the Romans to this Pope's memory. The Pope also built a chapel in St John Lateran's where he wished to be buried. Two of the columns in this chapel formally adorned the portico of the Pantheon of Agrippa. This is another of Cucherat's attempts at explanation.

A reference Columna is usually an allusion to the fact that one of the Colonna family would succeed to the Papacy.

BENEDETTO XIV	CLEMENTE XIII	CLEMENTE XIV	PIO VI
1740 1758	1758 1769	1769 1774	1775 1799
PROSPERO LAMBERTINI	CARLO REZZONICO	GIAN VINCENZO GANGANELLI	GIOVANNI ANGELO BRASCHI
PIO VII	LEONE XII	PIO VIII	GREGORIO XVI
1800 1823	1823 1829	1829 1830	1831 1846
BARNABA GREGORIO CHIARAMONTI	ANNIBALE DELLA GENGA	FRANCESCO SAVERIO CASTIGLIONI	BARTOLOMEO ALBERTO CAPPELLARI
PIO IX	LEONE XIII	S. PIO X	BENEDETTO XV
1846 1878	1878 1903	1903 1914	1914 1922
GIOVANNI M. MASTAI FERRETTI	GIOACCHINO PECCI	GIUSEPPE SARTO	GIACOMO DELLA CHIESA
PIO XI	PIO XII	GIOVANNI XXIII·	PAOLO VI
1922 1939	1939 1958	1958 1963	1963
ACHILLE RATTI	EUGENIO PACELLI	ANGELO GIUSEPPE RONCALLI	GIOVANNI BATTISTA MONTINI *fel. regnante*

82

ANIMAL RURALE
Animal of the field

BENEDICT XIV
1740 - 1758

Prospero Lorenzo Lambertini

Prospero was born in 1675 and at the age of nineteen he received the degrees of Doctor of Theology and Doctor of Canon and Civil Law. In 1727 he was made Bishop and in 1728 Cardinal. When Clement XII died the Conclave lasted for six months and the election then seemed no nearer than at the beginning. Cardinal Lambertini, who had been proposed as a compromise, addressed the Conclave saying: "If you wish to elect a saint, choose Gotti; a statesman, Aldabrandini; an honest man, elect me". Lambertini was chosen and took the name of Benedict XIV. He died in 1758.

There appears to be no reason for interpreting the legend as an allusion to the Pope's armorial bearings. Interpreters stress the fact that the Pope wrote away at his desk like a "plodding ox", which, according to the old writers, was typical of the persevering steady worker. (St Thomas Aquinas was called the dumb ox by his fellow students because he fed his mind and ruminated silently.)

ROSA UMBRIÆ
The rose of Umbria

CLEMENT XIII
1758 - 1769

Carlo Rezzonico

Carlo was born at Venice in 1693 and became Bishop of Padua in 1743. In 1747 he became a Cardinal and in 1758 he was elected Pope. He died in 1769.

The interpretations given to Malachy's legend appear somewhat far fetched; however, during his Pontificate he raised to the dignity of saints a great number of persons belonging to the Franciscan order, mystically called *Rosa Umbriæ*.

URSUS VELOX
The swift bear

CLEMENT XIV
1769 - 1774

Lorenzo (or Giovanni Vincenzo Antonio) Ganganelli

He was born in 1705. He received his education from the Jesuits of Rimini and at the age of nineteen he entered the order of the Franciscans. Clement XIII gave him the Cardinal's hat in 1759 and the Conclave of 1769 chose him to succeed Clement XIII. Under his pontificate the Jesuits were suppressed. He died in 1774.

Without producing any evidence, the American interpreter Robb states that the Pope's family coat of arms showed a running bear. However, with the death of Panvinio we lose much of the informations which helpe earlier interpreters.

Wion, O'Kelly and Cucherat try in vain to give a reasonable explanation of this legend. There is no bear in the arms of the Pope and to my mind it is unlikely that the imminent French revolution is typified in Malachy's description. This is again one of the instances where any interpretation would be purely guess work.

PEREGRINUS APOSTOLICUS
The pilgrim pope
P I U S   V I
1775 - 1799

GIOVANNI ANGELICO BRASCHI

Giovanni was born in 1717. He became Papal secretary in 1755 and Clement XIV made him a Cardinal in 1755. After this, he retired to the Abbey of Subiaco (of which he was Abbot) until his election in the same year. He died in 1799.

The legend is usually explained by the well known facts of the Pope's life. His extremely long Pontifical reign had led contemporary writers to refer to him as the Apostolic Pilgrim on Earth.

AQUILA RAPAX
A rapacious eagle

P I U S   V I I
1800 - 1823

BARNABA CHIARAMONTI

This pope was born in 1740 and his elevation to the Papacy was foretold, as Pius VII himself later related, by his mother, who in 1763 had entered the convent of Carmelites. Pius VI created him a Cardinal in 1786 and the Conclave elected him Pope in 1800. He died in 1823.

The Pope's pontificate was overshadowed by Napoleon whose emblem was the eagle.

CANIS ET COLUBER
A dog and a serpent

LEO XII
1823 - 1829

ANNIBALE DELLA GENGA

Born in 1760, Annibale became a Priest at the age of only twenty-three. In 1820 he was made Vicar of Rome and after Pius VII's death was elected to the Papacy. He died in 1829.

I think it is fair to say that if the order of two successive Popes could be reversed, the allusion to armorial bearings would fit perfectly. What better description for Leo XII than that which was given to Pius VII "*Aquila Rapax*" and how perfect would Pius VII have been described with the legend "*Custus Montium*" or "*Crux de Cruce*", if chance would have had it so.

Contrary to popular belief, the original manuscript of the Prophecies of Malachy has not been found in the Vatican Library. His Excellency Archbishop Cardinale instigated a thorough search for the manuscript at the Vatican. The sad fact is that there is no *record* of this manuscript being there or having been there. The many publications and additions to Malachy's prophecies since the middle of the sixteenth century do not concur exactly with the order of the Popes, particularly during the reigns of the antipopes. It is also reasonable to assume that the interpreters have relied largely on the works of their predecessors, adopting the same order of succession.

As matters stand Malachy's prophecy concerning Leo XII may be a reference to two of the Pope's most outstanding virtues: vigilance, which one associates with a dog; and prudence, commonly associated with the serpent.

VIR RELIGIOSUS
A religious man

PIUS VIII
1829 - 1830

Francesco Saverio Castiglioni

Francesco was born in 1761 and attended a Jesuit school. In 1800 Pius VII appointed him Bishop of Moltalto and he held various episcopal sees. As early as the Conclave of 1823 Castiglioni was among the candidates for the Papacy. Cardinal Wiseman relates that this Pope's elevation to the Papacy, as well as the name he was to assume, was predicted by Pius VII for, on a certain occasion, the Pope addressed Cardinal Castiglioni and said, "Your Holiness Pius VIII may one day settle this matter". At the election of 1829 he succeeded Pius VII and he died on the 1st December 1830.

Malchy's legend may refer to the fact (Religiosus) that the Pope had come from a family which was well known for its deep faith and that he was not the first Pope this family had given to the Church. Other interpreters have taken *Religiousus* to mean the same as Pius, thus foreshadowing his name.

DE BALNEIS ETRURIÆ
From the baths of Etruria

GREGORY XVI
1831 - 1846

Mauro, or Bartolomeo Alberto Cappellari

Mauro was born in 1765 and upon entering the Camaldolese Monastery of San Michele di Murano took the name Mauro. Three years later he was professed and ordained priest in 1787. In 1800

Dom Mauro became Abbot. In 1825 Leo XII created him Cardinal and Prefect of the Congregation and Propaganda. Following the death of Pope Pius VIII he was elected to the See of St Peter in 1831. He died in 1846.

Gregory XVI started his religious life in the order of Camaldolese which was founded in the thirteenth century in a locality called in Latin *Balneum,* in Etruria. Under the Pope's personal supervision the most exquisite discoveries were made during the Etruscan excavations. The museum which contains these discoveries of ancient Etruscan art was in fact called after his name the "Gregorian Museum". The Pope's armorial bearings show on the dexterside the arms of the Camaldolese.

CRUX DE CRUCE
The cross from a cross

PIUS IX
1846 - 1878

Giovanni Maria Mastai Ferretti

Giovanni Maria was born in 1792 and was admitted to the Pope's noble court in 1814. He was refused admission to the priesthood on the grounds that he suffered from epilepsy and proceeded to study theology at the Roman Seminary. His health was completely restored by 1819 when he was ordained Priest. By 1827 he was created Archbishop and in 1840 he was made a Cardinal. In 1846, two weeks after the death of Gregory XVI, Cardinal Mastai Ferretti was elected Pope.

The loss of his temporal power was only one of the many trials that filled the long pontificate of Pius IX. There was scarcely a country where the rights of the Church were not infringed upon. In many countries church property was confiscated, religious orders were expelled and Bishops imprisoned or banished. The height of these disturbances was reached during the Kulturkampf inaugurated in 1873. Pius IX is well remembered for ordaining to important ecclesiastical positions only such men as were famous for both piety and learning. Among the great Cardinals created by him were Wiseman and Manning for England, Cullen for Ireland and McCloskey for the United States. On the 29th September 1850 he re-established the Catholic hierarchy in England by erecting the Archdiocese of Westminster with twelve Suffragan Sees. He died in Rome on the 7th February 1878.

Although a reference to the cross reoccurs frequently in the prophecies, there is little doubt that Pius IX had to bear the heaviest cross yet to be inflicted upon the Papacy. The temporal powers of the Church had been drastically curtailed and the influence of the spiritual leader of the Catholic world reduced. There is no doubt that the House of Savoy, whose emblem is a cross, added greatly to the afflictions of this Pope.

LUMEN IN CŒLO
A light in the sky

LEO XIII
1878 - 1903

GIOACCHINO PECCI

Gioacchino was born in 1810 and became a Priest in 1837. In 1843 he was appointed a Nuncio and consecrated Archbishop. In 1853 Pius IX made him a Cardinal. The Conclave of 1878 elected him Pope.

Among the instances of Leo XIII's influence in the English speaking world may be mentioned the elevation of John Henry Newman to the Cardinalate, the beatification of forty English martyrs, two Encyclicals *Ad Anglos* of 1895 on the return to Catholic unity, and

Apostolicæ Curæ of 1896 on the known validity of Anglican Orders. In Ireland he created Archbishop McCabe a Cardinal and in the United States he founded the Apostolic Delegation in Washington in 1892. Leo XIII died on the 20th July 1903.

This is the first of Malachy's legends since 1590 which appears to be a straightforward allusion to the Pope's armorial bearings which shows a blazing star in his coat of arms. The same blazing comet has occurred already in the arms of Innocent VII and the prophet refers to it as *"sydus"*. It has often been suggested that if Malachy's legend concerning Leo XIII read *"sydus in cœlo"* it would be more convincing. However, the fact remains that *"Lumen in Cœlo"* is a fairly good description of the Papal coat of arms.

IGNIS ARDENS
The burning fire

PIUS X

1903 - 1914

GIUSEPPE SARTO

Giuseppe was born in 1835 and was ordained in 1858. In 1884 he was appointed Bishop of Mantoa and in 1893 he became Patriarch of Venice and a Cardinal. He was probably the most zealous propagandist of his time. Before all else, his efforts were directed to the promotion of piety among the faithful. After the death of Leo XIII Cardinal Sarto was elected Pope. He died in 1914.

Without wishing to over-stress the point, *"Ignis Ardens"* most aptly describes this Pope, whose zeal and endeavour were directed towards the spiritual renaissance of the Church he headed.

RELIGIO DEPOPULATA
Religion laid waste

BENEDICT XV
1914 - 1922

GIACOMO DELLA CHIESA

Born in 1854 he spent most of his life in the diplomatic service. In 1907 he became Archbishop of Bologna and in 1914 Cardinal and Pope. During the First World War the Pope made many attempts to bring about peace and to relieve suffering. He died in 1922.

The years of Pope Benedict's reign were overshadowed by the death of millions of Christians in World War I. 1917 saw the beginning of the Russian revolution which brought about the end of religious life in this formerly most Christian country.

Religio Depopulata is one of Malachy's prophecies which have unfortunately been fulfilled true to the letter of the word.

FIDES INTREPIDA
Unshaken faith

PIUS XI
1922 - 1939

ACHILLE RATTI

Achille Ratti was born in 1857. He was appointed Prefect of the Vatican Library in 1914, Papal Nuncio to Poland in 1919 and Cardinal Archbishop of Milan in 1921. Elevated to the Papacy in 1922 he faced the rise of Fascism and Communism in the Western world. He died in 1939.

Recent publications of Vatican documents show the tremendous pressure which was put on this Pope by the dictators of Italy and Germany. Again one could say that it was the Pope's *"Fides Intrepida"* — his unshaken faith — in what he believed to be right which may have prevented even greater hardship than that which befell the Catholic Church during his reign. His courage at which Hitler sneered and raged and before which Mussolini crumbled; his outspoken criticism against Fascism and Communism which upset the ruthless plans of the dictators, and his unshaken faith, all sustained the Church in a period of the most severe trials. Malachy's description appears to be a most fitting one for Pope Pius XI.

PASTOR ANGELICUS
An angelic shepherd

PIUS XII

1939 - 1958

EUGENIO PACELLI

Born in 1876 Eugenio Pacelli spent most of his career in the diplomatic service. From 1917 until 1929 he was Nuncio in Germany and in 1930 he became Cardinal Secretary of State. His elevation to the Papacy in 1939 was a matter of formality because no other person could have followed in the steps of his predecessor more aptly. Pius XII died in 1958.

Recent publications, particularly that by Pinchas Lapide (*The Last Three Popes and the Jews,* Souvenir Press, 1967) and the publication of the Vatican documents relating to the reign of Pius XII, have given to the world unshakable and irrefutable proof of this Pope's greatness and spirituality. He was in the truest sense of the word an Angelic Pastor to the flock committed to his care, and his flock were all those who suffered. In spite of the defamatory and scurrilous allegations published about him in such contemporary plays as *The Representative* by Rolf Hochhuth, Pius XII has emerged as one of the great Popes of all time. Although the contents of his visions have not yet become public knowledge there is little doubt that his affinity to the spiritual world was a very real and close one. The description *Pastor Angelicus* is most apt and one of the most descriptive ones in Malachy's prophecies.

PASTOR ET NAUTA
Pastor and mariner

JOHN XXIII
1958 - 1963

ANGELO GIUSEPPE RONCALLI

Born in 1881 Giuseppe Roncalli spent many years as Apostolic Delegate and Nuncio in Turkey, Greece, Bulgaria and France. In 1953 he was created a Cardinal and appointed Patriarch of Venice and in 1958 the Conclave elected him Pope. In 1962 he convened the second Vatican Council and his Encyclical *Pacem in Terris* (1963) is considered one of the greatest documents of our time. He died in 1963.

Pope John was the pastor of the world and perhaps more loved by Catholics and non-Catholics alike than any other Pope in history. Malachy's legend *Pastor et Nauta** points immediately to the See of Venice which indeed he occupied as Patriarch before his elevation to the Papacy.

---

* During the conclave the rumour circulated in Rome that Cardinal Spellman of New York, who was known to be very interested in the Prophecies of Malachy, had hired a boat, filled it with sheep and sailed up and down the river Tiber.

FLOS FLORUM
Flower of flowers

PAUL VI

1963 -

GIOVANNI BATTISTA MONTINI

Born in 1897 he worked with his predecessors in the papal Secretariat of State and became Pro-Secretary of State in 1952. He was appointed Archbishop of Milan and Cardinal in 1958. In 1963 the Conclave elected him Pope.

Malachy's legend appears to be an obvious allusion to the Pope's armorial bearings which show three fleurs-de-lis.

*   *   *

The following four prophecies have still to be fulfilled:

DE MEDIETATE LUNÆ
Of the half moon

This may be both an allusion to armorial bearings as well as an indication of some great event concerning those whose religious life is lived under the sign of the half moon. The speculations in which one could engage here are numerous, particularly at a time when the Middle East situation might well prove to be the most dangerous threat to peace in the present times. Such a conflict might well lead to a "Holy War" which would be fought under the half moon and would have devastating effects and repercussions on Muslim and Christians alike.

DE LABORE SOLIS
(a) From the toil of the sun
(b) Of the eclipse of the sun

The election of this Pope will probably take place within the next two decades. It is difficult to decide on an interpretation because the two different translations given above allow for two entirely different trends of thought. In the introduction I have already dismissed the possibility of Malachy's legend being a reference to Matthew, ch. 24 vv. 5-29, and as I have said before, this may well be an allusion to the armorial bearings of the person to be elected. However, in order to interpret Malachy's legend, if it were to be translated "of the eclipse of the sun", I have made some enquiries concerning those full eclipses of the sun between 1970 and 1990 and discovered that there will be sixteen eclipses within those twenty years. Eclipses are far too numerous to exclude ambiguity. The question here would be where this eclipse could be seen. Somehow it is unlikely that the place of the Conclave (Rome) qualifies, because the next eclipse visible in Central and Southern Europe will not take place until the 11th August 1999. However, if for example the Pope after next had been born in America in 1900, 1904, 1908, 1916, 1918 or 1925 and was to be elected to the See of St. Peter in 1972, 1977, 1979, 1981 or 1984, the coincidence of having been born and elected under a full eclipse of the sun visible in his country of origin would certainly be re-markable, although, in my opinion, not conclusive. One could narrow the margin even more to the actual day of the eclipse which, of course, would be striking if it were to happen in that manner.

De labore solis allows for more than just these two translations: the labouring sun is a sun that radiates. I do not think that within the next decades the Church will be progressive enough to elect a pope from the African countries which might be yet another explanation. It is, however, well known that the heraldic devices chosen by the princes of the Church are sometimes unusual to say the least.

I am therefore convinced there must be a youngish bishop bearing the blazing sun, probably amongst other heraldic devices, in his coat of arms. However, it stands to reason that it will not be the sun but his qualification and piety which will be the decisive factors that cause the Sacred College to elect him as successor to St. Peter.

GLORIA OLIVÆ
The glory of the olive

Olive branch has always been associated with peace and this description might have been most fittingly applied to Pope Pius XII as a reference to his coat of arms. There is little doubt that this legend can be more easily explained in the future than the one before.

Some medieval interpreters have gone out of their way to stress that Malachy in his prophecies does not specifically mention that no Popes shall reign between *Gloria Olivæ* and the last *Petrus Romanus;* nor on the other hand does he mention that there will be others.

The Order of St Benedict has claimed by tradition that this pope will come from within the Order. St Benedict himself has prophecied that before the end of the world comes about, his Order will triumphantly lead the Catholic Church in its fight against evil. The Order of St Benedict is also known as the OLIVETANS, which may well account for another interpretation of the prophecy.

PETRUS ROMANUS

The final legend is self-explanatory and Malachy concludes his short but fascinating prophecies as follow: —

> "In the final persecution of the Holy Roman Church there will reign Peter the Roman, who will feed his flock among many tribulations; after which the seven-hilled city will be destroyed and the dreadful Judge will judge the people".